'Sometimes a Christian book
tant. These game-changer b
theology and the practical b
is an important book. It hel
see it in the context of the incarnation and creation...
practical, moving and at times heartbreakingly honest. I cannot
recommend it highly enough.'

Revd Steve Morris, ordained minister and writer

Entertaining Angels

Living well with autism as a family, in society and in church

Cavan Wood

Authentic

First published 2022 by Authentic Media Limited,
PO Box 6326, Bletchley, Milton Keynes, MK1 9GG.
authenticmedia.co.uk

British Library Cataloguing in Publication Data
A catalogue record for this book is available from the British Library.
ISBN: 978-1-78893-073-4
978-1-78893-074-1 (e-book)

Content advice provided by Autism Bedfordshire, October 2021,
reflecting current understanding of, and use of language about, autism.

Cover design by Natalie Wunn

Contents

Preface

There have been very few books written about autism from a Christian point of view. My intention in writing this one is to explain what autism is and to encourage society, the church and individuals to give appropriate support.

This comes from my experience as the father of an autistic child. The stories in this book are fictionalised versions of events or feelings that have happened to my family, so they contain the truth of experience but some invention to allow my family distance and to universalise their meanings.

Whether you know someone who is autistic or would like to be better informed about how autism affects people, I hope there are ideas and suggestions that could help you become more aware of a condition which shapes at least (a conservative estimate) one million people in the UK.

The church can be a vital part of making sure that all are treated with love and dignity. This is a call to action. The title, *Entertaining Angels*, is vital. Just like Abraham, we could meet angels in autistic people, messengers of God who speak the truth and challenge us in many ways. If we embraced that way of seeing things, it would be transformative.

Cavan Wood

Author's Note

The language we use about autism

There is a debate among those who have autism about how to address their state. Some professionals have used the expression 'a person with autism', as they are trying to show the value they perceive in the individual, not reducing them to a condition.

However, many autistic people prefer to use the description 'autistic', as they see that their condition is something that does define them, something they do not see as limiting and that they feel should be embraced. Increasingly, professionals are talking about autistic spectrum condition (ASC) rather than autistic spectrum disorder (ASD).

When dealing with autism, it is important that we speak and act in a way which does not reinforce stereotypes and in any way offend others. We should have a discussion about language with the individual where possible to see what they believe is appropriate.

Words are important as they contain the values we wish to communicate. For a Christian, the most important value is that all people – autistic or not – are made in the image of God.

Prologue: A Diagnosis

Our son. It is only about him.

Not me, him.

Why couldn't I focus on that? I needed to focus on that, I really did, but it did not come easily to me.

Trying to make his life a success. To let him know he is loved. That was what mattered now, wasn't it? Not me or my feelings.

Autism?

'The triad of impairments for autism needed for diagnosis were all satisfied,' the doctors said.

I don't even really know what it means.

But I know how it feels.

Not a word, but a sentence, a judgement, a label.

What were we going to do?

Could we do anything? Would we be able to help him?

The specialist had said something about how we could 'unlock his possibilities' if we created the right conditions; if we argued for our child, getting him the support that he needed; if we valued him and made the rest of the world believe that he could be someone, could achieve something.

Did I have enough imagination to see this? He was going to need me to believe. He was going to need me to think that things could happen.

So there we were, sitting listening to the specialist after they had done all the tests. Tom was eight years old.

'We think that your son is on the autistic spectrum,' said the specialist. 'He seems to show the types of behaviour that make this highly likely.'

I looked at my wife. What did this mean? This word – autism. In that moment, it seemed terrifying.

'Why?' I clearly looked and felt confused. 'I mean, how did you come to this conclusion?'

My wife sighed. She had been telling me of her concerns about Tom's behaviour for months. 'He is autistic. Let them explain.'

The specialist continued: 'We cannot be sure, but we think that it is tending in that direction. His lack of co-ordination and his slowness to acquire language are both pointers to the autistic spectrum. We need to put things in place so that he gets all the help he can. We will need to review the situation in a year or so.'

Were we being told that we had a disabled son? What did that mean? Is disabled the PC word?

So I asked the question that I began to realise was almost impossible to answer: 'Is he very far on the spectrum? I mean, is he one of the most severe cases?' I wanted some definition, something to hold on to.

The doctor was not going to give a simple 'yes' or 'no', it seemed. He wanted to live in a world of ifs and buts.

'So he might not be autistic at all?' I tried to press them further. I had to know, one way or the other.

The specialist said, 'I think it unlikely. He seems to fit many of the descriptors that match the spectrum. The question is how much. Will he be able to be taught in a special school or will the provision of special educational needs within the state system be enough? We cannot tell you at this moment. We have to do a more long-term study so that we can prepare him for going to school.'

My wife said, 'Thanks, doctor.'

'Thank you,' replied the specialist.

'Thank you,' I said.

Thanks. For what exactly?

We got up to leave. As we walked towards our son, I gripped my wife's hand and whispered into her ear, 'It will be all right. We can do this together, we can, we really can.'

She grabbed hold of Tom's hand and began to cry. 'I hope so. I hope so. But, Simon, you cannot know. No one can.'

We left the consulting room and walked out of the health centre to the car park, with our son between us. Words of consolation were not said again. In fact, there was a silence where both of us felt that we could not speak.

We seemed to grip our son's hands very tightly, as if hoping that could change things. What was there to say? We had tried to offer each other reassurance, but were not convincing the other or ourselves.

I could not believe that the diagnosis was right. How could my son be on the autistic spectrum? Yes, he found speech difficult, but didn't a lot of boys find learning to speak very difficult? He did seem to have a repetitive speech pattern when he did speak. But repetition is how you learn language, isn't it?

I felt that I could explain everything about Tom better than the so-called experts. I was his dad – I knew him better, didn't I?

Perhaps we needed to see some more specialists and they might not agree with the diagnosis? Perhaps the specialists we had seen had been wrong. Yet I felt I was trying to lie to myself. Time to face the truth.

'Say something, Simon, for goodness' sake!' my wife screamed at me. 'The one time I want you to say something, you are quiet. Speak!'

I felt a tear go down my cheek as I said: 'I can't. I can't. I want to, but I can't. I don't know what to think, I don't think I have any idea what to say.'

What we did not know then was that the diagnosis was going to be the beginning of a journey that would surprise, frustrate and delight us.

Reflection

After reading the story of diagnosis, think about these questions.

- What would you say to the parents about what happened to them?
- How could the church help them?
- How might God be found in this?

Prayer

Father, we pray for those families who are seeking diagnosis for autism. Give the doctors wisdom and help parents to understand their children's needs. Give all the grace and the patience they need to see the reality of autism. Help them to deal with the changes that they will have to face.

Amen

Part One

What Do We Mean by 'Autism'?

1

An Explanation of Autism

A friend once asked me the question: 'What is more difficult to live with – a broken arm or a broken mind?' Is autism a broken mind?

The model of autism as a matter of mental health is being rejected, but it is a condition that can lead to mental health issues. A bone can – on most occasions – be reset and restored. There is no cure for autism – despite many thinking there is.

The word 'autism' comes from the Greek word *autos*, which means 'self'. This term had previously been used in connection with people suffering from schizophrenia as they seemed to be locked away from the real world. We need to examine first how we got to our modern understanding of autism.

Sigmund Freud

When you look at the study of the mind, you always have to start in the modern era with Sigmund Freud. You could say that all our thinking about the brain and mental health has been either an acceptance or a rejection of his writings.

Some writers have been dismissive of him, such as Hans Eysenck, who once said that the trouble with Freud was that he had worked with a bunch of Viennese neurotics and thought that the whole world was like them!

We are all guilty to some extent of being limited in our thinking by the historical and emotional context we live in. Freud's theories about the relationship with the mother causing mental illness certainly influenced a whole generation of psychologists. For Freud, this relationship not only caused mental illness, but led to religion and our political structures. It was a total theory (that is, it was used to describe all of reality) and that is a problem with it. A total theory *cannot* describe all reality. When you try to make something fit it, problems arise when that item does not conform to the underlying assumption.

It is interesting to observe that, where Freud is still revered, people with autism are treated less well. Recent surveys in France have suggested that over-reliance on Freud has led to the somewhat regressive attitudes and the lack of support from the state with regard with autism. These are now beginning to change, but slowly.

From a Christian theological analysis, Freud is essentially reductionist, that is, he has one theory and reduces all experience to that. Having a total theory will ultimately mean that you either miss information that does not fit your ideas, or you will try to reduce the importance of others' ways of looking at reality. His use of information and ideas was selective, to build and reinforce his thinking.

The idea of creation where the Creator God creates all of the differing realities we inhabit suggests that we can examine the world through a number of different lenses – psychological, sociological, political, genetic for example, all part of a jigsaw. It cannot be reduced to one thing only. However good psychology is, it is only one facet of the story of any one person and of our culture.

We have a God who has created many different layers to the reality we see and given us the brains to think through the multidimensional nature of that truth. As we are fallen sinners, we can never fully understand the reality we face because we are partial due to both sin and the time we live in but, by a combination of different methods coming together, we can begin to explain the world we face.

In this way, the idea of the autistic spectrum fits with the idea of creation, as it does not lead us to diminish a wide range of experiences to one simple and obviously stereotypical explanation, but allows for a variety of types and explanations.

The term 'autism' was first used in 1911 by Eugen Bleuler, but he applied it to the social isolation felt by schizophrenic patients. It was to take our next thinker to apply it in a way we now recognise.

Leo Kanner

The first person to identify autism as a separate condition was Leo Kanner in 1943. He coined the term 'early infantile autism'. He was studying people who he saw were completely disengaged from the world, living in their own head and finding communication with the outside world difficult, if not impossible. He saw that each individual was different, which could be seen as the beginning of the idea of an autistic spectrum.

Kanner's work first appeared in a paper called 'Autistic Disturbances of Affective Contact'.[1] He used the now controversial term, 'refrigerator mother', claiming that a cause of autism was the emotional coldness of the mother of an autistic child. He does add that others can cause this as well – including fathers – and he notices that, in some of the cases, the marriages of the parents were cold and dysfunctional. Yet the cold-hearted father was not highlighted as much as the mother – a sign perhaps of the post-Freudian obsessions of psychiatry or the sexism of culture Kanner was working in?

If only the child had had emotional warmth and care, then they would have been different. His thesis was not disproved until the early 1970s, meaning a whole generation of parents was made to feel it was their fault that their children were not developing emotionally, mentally and socially. Wrongly-attached blame had consequences for the wellbeing of both those with autism and those caring for them.

As Christians, we accept that we inevitably do ruin our relationships with others by sin, but it was simplistic and we now know plain wrong to blame the development of autism on a problem with the parents. It might be that the parents of autistic children blame themselves but essentially the causes of autism are largely thought to be genetic. In some ways, this is much harder to accept than a blame 'explanation'.

We need to realise that it is how we react to the person with autism that can be sinful, for example, when we get irritated about their obsessions or angry in response to their anger meltdowns. We will need the grace of patience and forbearance in many situations. These may be for many of us real battles, but they will not only help the autistic person but will also make us what God wants us to be – closer to Christ.

Kanner's work was a study of eleven children, eight of whom were male and three were female. (Many theorists have argued that autism is essentially a male condition, but Kanner was the first to use this term and was able to identify it in females as well.)

One of the cases Kanner looked at was a child he called Donald F. He described the child as having obsessions, finding it difficult to talk to others, having temper tantrums and being withdrawn from the world – some of the classic indicators of autism as it was once understood.

Kanner thought that the obsessions the child had were the consequences of behaviour learnt from their parents. It is true that we can influence our children's preferences, but the level of obsession in autism is not possible to teach. Although children are a reflection of their parents, they are not our puppets – they are individuals, made in the image of God. They do make their own choices, even if they are limited.

We should remember that Kanner's work was done before the rise of genetics, which locates the origins of the condition in a place other than the role of parental behaviour. He is important still as a descriptor of the condition, but his analysis of its causes needs to be treated with caution. Blame is not helpful or appropriate to the situation.

Hans Asperger

At the same time as Kanner was writing, Hans Asperger was practising as a doctor, doing his research in Europe. There is now evidence to suggest that he gave information to the Nazis about his patients' conditions, which may have led to their deaths in euthanasia clinics and in concentration camps. (There is also some evidence that he may have saved many too.) However, again this should not lead to us rejecting his theories out of hand as they do provide some good descriptors of what is going on with some people.

He was dealing with what is now sometimes called 'high-functioning autism'. Asperger referred to the children he studied as 'little professors'. The 1970s term 'Asperger's syndrome' is applied to people who seem to be high-functioning – in other words, cognitively able and articulate but showing other characteristics we link to autism.

Some theorists believe that Asperger's thinking might have come out of his own experience. Little Hans had found it hard to make friends, being considered a little odd by his peers. He would learn vast chunks of poetry, which he would take delight in reciting to people. He liked to refer to himself in the third person. 'Hans's thinks' was a phrase that he often used, to refer to his thoughts. So was his study a thinly disguised autobiography or an attempt to understand himself? In part it may be. This need not make it wrong – but it does give it a context.

Asperger's study of a small group of boys led him to coin the term 'little professors', as he felt they acted as if they were academics, talking about their issues, their obsessions, in the way that an academic might do. He noticed the following characteristics in the people he studied:

- They seemed to lack empathy with others. What others thought or felt was of little or no interest to them. They needed to talk about their agenda.
- They seemed to have little ability to form friendships or understand the depth at which a relationship worked.
- Their conversations tended to be one-sided, and if another person was able to move the conversation on, they would ignore this and take it back to where they wanted it to be.
- They had an intense absorption in a special interest – for example trains and train timetables.
- They were characterised as having clumsy movements.

The term 'Asperger's syndrome' was coined, after he had died, by Lorna Wing. Given the controversy about his possible involvement with Nazism, it is not as widely used today.

Both Kanner's and Asperger's work has been criticised as they looked at small samples of children who were predominantly from academic families, thus giving the idea that it was a condition that was linked to intelligence. Clearly, autism cuts across all the different levels of intelligence and class. The methods of Kanner and Asperger are seen by some as not objective enough, as they themselves were affected by the conditions they were describing.

The widening of the autistic community to see Asperger's syndrome as a facet of autism might well have broadened the base on which to campaign for change.

Bruno Betthelheim

Bruno Bettelheim developed Kanner's idea that autism was an emotional disorder that developed in some children because of psychological harm from their emotionally distant, 'refrigerator mothers'. Bettelheim wrote extensively and was on television a lot promoting his theory in the 1960s and 1970s.

The writer Richard Pollack suggested Bettelheim had wrongly presented evidence and created a theory which was flawed.[2] Bettelheim's set of ideas had a huge influence – making a whole generation of parents ashamed and confused, perhaps leading many of them to not seek the help they should have had to support their children.

Bernard Rimland

In 1964 Bernard Rimland, who was father to a son with autism, presented the arguments that autism is not related to the parent–child bond being in some way dysfunctional or cold, but is a biological condition unrelated to parental interactions. He founded the Autism Society of America for parents to have a voice against the 'refrigerator mother' theory. Slowly but surely, he won the argument against the development of Kanner's theory by Bettleheim. Here again, autobiography informed theory – Rimland saw that a flawed theory damaged his own son and others too.

The problem of a total theory

The belief that one total theory can describe all of reality – everything is psychological, for example – is simplistic. We need to use many different lenses to see the glory of the created order, especially the complex creation that human beings are. Perhaps the concept of a total theory about autism was formed by people who universalised their own experience. While this could bring insights, it was to be the mother of an autistic child who first articulated the way we see autism now.

All who are the parents of autistic children may well find themselves the researchers in this area. Yet we know now that what may be true of one person with autism may not be true of all.

Accepting that all people are unique, we still observe more than has been known or understood before about the way people function. We as Christians should embrace these insights and not reject them. Everyone is made in the image of God and needs to have their dignity respected. Full acceptance of all aspects of human beings, tempered by respect, should help us understand other people better.

Lorna Wing and Judith Gould

It is the work of Lorna Wing and Judith Gould that has become important to how we understand autism now. Wing coined the phrase 'Asperger's syndrome' as she had been reading his work and developing her theories from him. With Gould, she developed the concept of the triad of impairments – social interaction, communication and imagination – that are used to talk about the characteristics of autism. Their work rejected talk of a cure for the condition. It was the basis of seeing autism as a spectrum condition, not a one-size fits all phenomenon.

One of the important things about Lorna Wing's work was that it was not just theoretical; it was personal. Her daughter Susie had had screaming fits and, at the age of three, was diagnosed as autistic. With the help of her husband, Wing discovered the writing of Asperger who had largely been forgotten by researchers. She read and began to reflect on what he had said. She could see some strengths and weaknesses, believing that he had described some parts well but she rejected some of his conclusions.

Lorna Wing helped to set up the National Autistic Society in the early 1960s in the UK. By the 1970s, she and Gould were beginning to challenge the received orthodoxy about autism.

Wing helped Asperger's syndrome to be recognised internationally. This led to it being classified as a condition by the World Health Organisation, which in turn led many more countries to embrace more proactive policies to help people with the condition.

She was wary of the all-embracing definitions, declaring: 'One of my favourite sayings is that nature never draws a line without smudging it. We need to see each child as an individual.' She drew attention to the variations of behaviour and ability among people with the same diagnosis of autism.

Wing began to say that, rather than just being about limitations, there could be strengths in the condition. Quoted in *The Guardian* in 2011, she reflected, 'I do believe you need autistic traits for real success in science and the arts, and I am fascinated by the behaviours and personalities of musicians and scientists.'[3] Her work began to remove the stigma and suggest some possibilities, strengths even, that could be seen in autistic people.

She saw some forms of autism as giving an advantage as they encouraged single-mindedness, an obsession-driven mind which leads to scientific advancement or some great works of art. Instead of seeing it as abnormal, perhaps we need to realise that much of human culture owes its existence to those it would have written off at one time. Some of those 'obsessives' were the inventors, the thinkers, the authors and artists who have made our lives better.

Simon Baron-Cohen

Simon Baron-Cohen is one of the most important current researchers and writers on autism and is a professor at Cambridge University. His interest in autism was stimulated after he had graduated from Oxford University, when he worked in a special school for autistic children. He has been sceptical about the way in which Asperger's syndrome has become seen as a variant of autism, rather than as a condition itself.

In his *Mindblindness: An Essay on Autism and Theory of Mind*, Baron-Cohen suggests that the fundamental problem for people with autism is that their minds are unable to predict what others may or may not be thinking, which is something he believes that the rest of the population do all the time, without necessarily consciously thinking about it.[4]

He proposed what he called the 'extreme male brain' theory. This suggested that autism has some characteristics that we associate with males, which are pronounced in people with autism.

Baron-Cohen identified two categories in particular:

1. *Systemising* He saw this as the desire to follow rules and to make things into systems; he believed this a more common trait in males. We might link this with mathematicians, who seek to find order and meaning in numbers. Baron-Cohen sees autistic people as trying to do this to a higher degree than most people. A person with a high IQ with autism may become an authority on a time in history or science. An autistic person with a lower intellect may collect objects like stones and arrange them by type.

2. *Empathising* This is the drive to understand how other people think and feel, and to try to anticipate how they react to events or in conversations. This is normally seen as a female characteristic and Baron-Cohen believed less likely to be found in autistic people.

Baron-Cohen suggested that high levels of foetal testosterone during pregnancy leads to the development of this tendency. It may be that the brains of people with autism grow faster and have some developmental changes as a consequence.

He has said that autism should be seen as a disability or a different way of thinking and not as a disease that needs to be cured. Moving away from the 'disease' model has been important to help lead to acceptance and not exclusion. Autistic people are not 'ill' but have a different wiring to the brain.

He has made some great discoveries and even those who do not agree with all of his ideas can see the thoroughness of his research. He has suggested that autism could come to be seen as one of a number of different paths along which people develop. The stigma that can be attached to it would be removed if it was seen as one variant of humanity, in the way that left-handedness is.

Reflections on the theorists' work

Sometimes, there has been a reaction to autism which sees it as a kind of superpower. There are still genuine issues of understanding and personal/social/communication limitations which need to be taken seriously. (A good example of this is the US television series *Touch*, which sees an autistic, non-verbal boy as the key to understanding the end of the world.) We need to make sure that we neither demonise nor exalt people on the autistic spectrum: let us treat them all as people of dignity, whom God created and chose to love.

We can be so concerned with trying to avoid the problem of labelling and limiting people that we end up in an opposite place where we allow for more prospects than are actually possible. We need to not surrender to despair or to false dreams: we need to face reality for ourselves and for the autistic.

One of the questions I have is about the provision of a diagnosis of autism. Do middle-class professional parents benefit most from the system as they are more able to 'play' it? Do they tend to be less deferential to authority and therefore are prepared to be 'pushy' to get the support they feel their children deserve?

An article in the *American Journal of Public Health* suggested in 2017 that diagnosis of autism for a child was frequently tied to the socioeconomic background of the parents.[5] Its study was looking at statistics over a decade and concluded that the higher up the socioeconomic scale they came, the more likely they were to get a diagnosis of autism. Lower down, parents either did not get such help or were left without appropriate support.

The church needs to be on the side of justice. If there are members of our community who are not getting the help from the system they deserve, then we must do all we can to support and empower them. We should not walk by on the other side of this or forget the urgency of the parable of the sheep and goats, which calls us to think about supporting our brothers and sisters in need.

Neurodiverse and neurotypical

As the study of autism has developed, the use of language has changed. Two terms that are being widely used now are neurodiverse and neurotypical. The word 'neurodiverse' refers to people who have a different way of thinking and behaving, trying to avoid the model of disability but to suggest difference. This encompasses those on the autistic spectrum and with other conditions.

'Neurotypical' refers to anyone who does not have a condition like autism. They think and feel in a way that is broadly similar to the majority of people. This language is much better and more helpful than contrasting autism with 'normal'.

These terms also suggest that there is not necessarily a huge gap between those who are autistic and those who have Asperger's syndrome.

The Government Equalities Office of the UK in 2014 recommended a social model of autism with an emphasis on diversity rather than disability.[6]

Rejecting the so-called medical reasons has enabled progress to happen. Autism isn't a sickness, but it affects interactions and perception.

Who is responsible for autism?

Over the years, people have sought out things or people to blame for autism, to help deal with something that seems unfair to some. Randomness makes it appear even more unfair. However, the reasons put forward have been diverse and most have ultimately proved to be dead ends.

Is it the MMR (mumps, measles and rubella) jab or 'refrigerator mothers'? Could it be foetal testosterone? Most such ideas have been decisively rejected or subjected to intense debate.

Although autism is believed to arise from combinations of genetic and environmental factors, no 'autism gene' as such has been identified. Medical professionals do offer parents of autistic people genetic tests. But are the results worth knowing or not? Could receiving such information lead parents to blame themselves or their partners for the condition? Can a relationship survive that type of pressure?

If people go down this line, they have to ask themselves a number of questions: what is the purpose of this test? Is it to provide information? To what end? Autism is not a life-limiting condition like Huntington's disease. Do sons and daughters without the condition need to know the source of their sibling's condition? Other family members may have similar characteristics. Yet each child is a unique genetic coming together of the parents.

If it was possible to make a direct and clear connection between some genetic feature of two parents and their autistic child, would those parents be entitled to be told? To my mind, this is a dangerous temptation. Do we want to remove the diversity of humanity by what seems to be a return to the idea of eugenics? This might create unnecessary fear every bit as much as helping parents to make informed decisions.

If we could prove autism had a direct and clear genetic basis, and could be tested for during pregnancy, what might follow? How do different cultures deal with it, and where do you draw the line? Isn't this just the politics of the master race put into a more affirming way, made to seem helpful and respectful of the difficulties that parents might face?

Do we have the right to genetically remove those people who are neurologically different? Or should we not accept diversity and learn from it? Conformity is not a virtue nor does it respect the nature of the creation. We are all made in the image of God, but that image is expressed in billions of ways.

I don't know. These are mysteries that are best left to God in his wisdom.

Is being the parent of an autistic child a test from God? I am not sure that is a very helpful way to look at it, though I can understand the emotional and spiritual reasons why some people feel like that. I am not convinced that God causes suffering, but he can certainly use it if it is offered to him. We can at times over-spiritualise what are just human difficulties.

Reflection

If autism is a form of suffering, what can it teach us?

Think of it this way. We are like a block of stone (C.S. Lewis once said) and the knocks we have in life can be painful but they are also the process whereby the sculptor might just make a thing of great beauty. The knocks hurt but they are essential to getting to the greatest piece of art. Will we become better people from experiencing suffering? Some people do, but some turn into much less than themselves, becoming selfish and self-obsessed.

However, surely it is the suffering of the autistic person that should be our centre of attention, not just ours as the parents or family related to the person. How do we support people who will never be able to communicate the pain of their experiences? How do we support the person who finds the modern world a source of anxiety in all of its facets?

What we need to avoid here is having a discussion about evil. The gospel is not about karma – it is about grace. The gospel is not about making people feel needlessly wrong. The autistic person is not as they are because of the acts or sins of others.

We do not want to return to the blame culture of 're-frigerator mothers'. Any explanation of autism that seems to provoke a karma-like response is always going to be rejected. Yet karma is a default position we could go to. Saying that actions have consequences is not true of a condition like autism, although for some, it will seem so.

I know that I am by nature an impatient person, but I don't think that as a consequence I have become a parent to a child with autism to make me learn something about my own level of sin. That is almost an incidental thing; it is the needs of the one I love with autism that I need to be more receptive to. If you are a parent of an autistic child, don't make autism about you. Find support to help you to carry on, but think and pray for the other most.

Consider the message of Job: well, it might be a test or it is just what happens as we are human. But above all, God is in control and God will speak to us right in the middle of the chaos we face.

'Out of the storm the Lord spoke', says Job 38:1 (gnb). It isn't in easy places that God meets his people – it is in deserts, in storms, in seas. Why do we think we can only meet God in the sunshine? We should meet him everywhere – in the depths and the heights. We do not get a free pass on suffering if we are believers.

Why would God do this to him, one of his servants? But should he think that he had a right to be protected from the way the world was?

Simon did a test and it seemed to show that he too was on the autistic spectrum. He suspected that the test was biased. How could he be on that spectrum? He had never had any sense that he fitted the descriptors. Tom's problem – was him, writ large? That frightened him. Why was this suffering happening to him? It was not fair.

He believed that he knew himself inside out. This was suggesting that he did not even understand himself. That seemed to be completely unlikely – or was it a truth that he did not wish to own, that he dared not admit to himself?

There are many types of suffering and it can be argued that being the parent of a disabled child is a form of suffering. They might:

- Face the disapproving looks of people on trains or other public transport.

- Endure teachers who don't understand or would prefer they took their children to another school where they wouldn't be such a problem.
- Choose a school that does not understand the condition and writes a negative report or gives a destructive label without a moment's thought for the possible consequences for the person or their family.
- Have to cope with the misunderstandings of grandparents who do not really comprehend what autism is.
- Have a doctor who refuses to treat their child as he thinks the child is deliberately misbehaving.

These can be painful and difficult moments. Suffering offered to God will be redemptive; it can bring meaning and give insight. We do not seek suffering, but if we bring it to God he will redeem it. This will not make it easier but it can then go on to help others on their difficult paths.

Prayer

Father, we pray for those who are confused and troubled following a diagnosis of autism in a person they love. Help them to see not just problems but possibilities, to find you in even the most difficult places or times.
Amen

2

The Signs of Autism

There have been many attempts to give descriptors to the autism spectrum disorder (ASD), sometimes referred to as the autism spectrum condition (ASC). This being defined as a spectrum or constellation inevitably means that not all people with the condition will have the same characteristics. Let us start by looking at the behavioural characteristics frequently observed.

Behavioural characteristics

Sticking rigidly to routines

Perhaps there is an insistence on routines. This may sound trivial but can be quite imprisoning, as we shall see. For example, a child who has to have chips on a Friday evening and gets genuinely worried if that does not happen. Another child will not be happy to do anything after school, preferring to return to the 'safe' environment of the home. Another child has to watch the same DVD over and over again.

Resistance to change

There's an old joke, 'How many Anglicans does it take to change a light bulb?' The answer is 'Change?!' Ironically, this represents the spirit of mind which can be shown in those who are on the autism spectrum. The importance of an unbending routine can be seen as a way to try and find an escape from anxiety. Most of us are unsettled by change: autistic people can display a more intense version of a typical human experience. Change can bring chaos: therefore you fight it to stay calm and safe.

Displaying repetitive behaviour

Patterns of repetitive behaviour may occur in speech or in bodily movements, which can test the patience of those who do not realise what is happening. Think for a moment. We repeat things if we have enjoyed something – such as repeating the punch line to a joke we particularly enjoyed. We reread a novel or re-watch a film several times – so what a person with ASD is doing could be argued to be a heightened version of what a neurotypical person does. However, those around the autistic person may find this quite wearing as it will be done many more times than normally expected. It is part of a calming process; by doing a gesture over and over or revisiting behaviour, the autistic person is attempting to calm themselves.

Challenging behaviour

Frustration or feeling overwhelmed might lead a person with autism to lash out violently or have angry outbursts. This is behaviour that can frighten other people. Remember too that it might actually frighten the autistic person as well, as they may fear or reflect on the consequences after the event or lack any understanding of their emotions.

Unusually focused interests

Those on the autistic spectrum can sometimes retain large amounts of information which seems impressive. One person will be able to tell you all the British prime ministers since they began, or the football scores, or the chart places of a music act; these information interests can be difficult to cope with if you are not interested yourself; bus or train timetables or the colours of cars may not be of particular interest to anyone else.

Rituals and obsessions

There is a thin line between rituals and obsessions. A ritual is something we like to do at a certain time or in a certain way, such as eating a particular breakfast cereal, listening to a particular radio programme or following a football team. Much of the behaviour we see in autism is a magnified version of what many of us do. Many autistic children, for example, will fixate on model trains, Peppa Pig, Lego or Doctor Who. One child has to see a particular Thomas the Tank Engine DVD every day.

Experts believe that these bring comfort and calm to autistic people. Now, we need to think about how we can use some of these interests, for example, Lego therapy. This encourages children to work together to build Lego figures or models in order to help them develop their social skills. It also helps to encourage social imagination – thinking of ideas and trying to make them happen, a skill set that we all need but is often underdeveloped in autistic people.

This characteristic was well shown in an episode of *The A Word* about the need for routines. Joe (the autistic child) has to have a walk, to listen to an iPod with his songs playing, and to be allowed not to answer some questions until his family have answered his pop trivia questions.

Routines help autistic people deal with the anxiety they experience. To me, this is where autism isn't an example of a disability but about intensifying human experience. Most of us have routines and feel uneasy if we have them challenged. Let us be honest with ourselves – this is where I think there is more common ground than neurotypical people allow for.

Remember that an obsession can help an autistic person to deal with anxiety, as well as the cause of it if that is what they are obsessing about. This is an area where we need to be most helpful. How far do you allow the obsession? Some seem to think that tolerating it is almost analogous to helping an addict get off drink or drugs by letting them have 'just a little', but that is not the most helpful approach to the issue. Instead we should cherish those behaviours that induce calmness while also encouraging the development of other interests.

Repetitive or stereotyped body movements

Actions such as hand-flapping or spinning are believed to help reduce the anxiety levels that a person with autism can feel. Called 'stimming', the actions seem to help lessen the tension, as they act as a physical release to the anxiety the child is handling. Trying to stop them, encouraging them to move away from using them, or actively discouraging them might lead to some increase in stress for an autistic person. We need to realise that this behaviour can be beneficial, reducing the likelihood of other problems.

Dealing with unusual behaviour

It can be difficult to deal with the obsessions that are part of the autistic condition.

Tom spent a morning lining up all the engines from Thomas the Tank Engine in an order he believed to be correct. They had to be put into a sequence of colour – from darkest to lightest. This patterning was a sign of his autism.

He would have to eat off the same plate and have the same implements in order to be able to be relaxed at meal times. If anything was in the wrong order, he would scream. He would not rest until the same stories were read in the same order each night. By the end of the first couple of months, Simon and Carol could recite all the words of 'We're Going on a Bear Hunt' or 'Duck in the Truck'. The order to the words and the pictures mattered a great deal to Tom. Whether he understood the meanings behind them was another matter. The doctors seemed to think that he was going to have difficulty learning to write and perhaps actually begin to lose some of the words that he had. No one seemed to have much confidence in Tom's future.

Pica

Unusual sensory behaviours include sniffing objects and chewing normally inedible things. This is called 'pica'. This is done to seek to find some comfort. There is reassurance in the familiar. It may also be linked to sensory sensitivity, i.e. sensory seeking behaviour.

Sensory sensitivities

There can be sensory sensitivities such as avoiding the noises made by hairdryers, vacuum cleaners and other machinery. These may seem louder to a person with autism than to other people. They can be very sensitive to physical pain, which makes things like injections much more difficult. A greater sensitivity to light means that bright, fluorescent lights can often lead to sensory overload. We need to be aware of these possibilities and make changes where we can.

Specific ordering of items

Some autistic people may wish to line things up. For example, a young child could arrange a collection of books on a shelf in a certain way which cannot be challenged, as the plan brings some order into their world. Another child might have to display models or magazines in a particular order. Disruption of this pattern can cause distress.

Self-injury

We need to keep an especially careful eye on our young and teenage autistic children to prevent them from developing habits of self-harm. We know that many teenage girls who have anorexia may also be autistic. It has been noticing the existence of self-harm among teenage girls that has led to the very late-in-the-day diagnosis of autism that some have been given.

We need to encourage all people to see themselves as valuable and to see themselves as in the image of God – capable of love, creativity and being spiritual. We need to ask if self-harm is really a sign of autism, as much as the harm caused by other issues.

Social characteristics

The second category to the condition is in connection with social characteristics.

Friendships

There are difficulties in making and keeping friends. An autistic person may fail to understand what the nature of friendship is or be unable to judge where they are in a relationship.

Communication differences

Not being able to respond to facial and non-verbal (body language) cues, and lack of communication through eye contact, facial expressions and gestures are common characteristics. This can be deeply frustrating for other people, who feel they are being ignored or rejected, but are not meant that way by the autistic person. Psychologists tell us that we read a great deal from the body language and the facial expressions we are presented with and, if they don't fit our expected patterns, this can be difficult for us.

A parent may not realise that their son does not look at them directly until it is pointed out in a diagnosis session. It may be that some autistic people will make eye contact with close members of their family as their levels of anxiety might be lower than around other non-family members. Many families adjust to their autistic relative unconsciously and will have to be shown what is going on by a third party, which can sometimes be quite disturbing, as we tend to feel if there is one thing we understand, it is the people closest to us! Those 'funny little ways' that our children have could be more significant than we think.

Aloofness

People on the autistic spectrum can appear to be distant or aloof as they have difficulties sharing their own interests and entering into the activities of others. This is not the self-obsession of the rude (as some might feel it) but a genuine trait of autistic personalities. They may as a consequence feel happier with their own company than that of others. They can misjudge when there is a need to take turns, such as in a conversation, which can make things very difficult for them or those caring for them, as this will foster a sense of frustration.

Difficulties with empathy

Autistic people will not necessarily anticipate how another person is feeling and can therefore say or do the wrong thing. They will not understand that true communication is a dialogue and not a monologue. They can become very fixed in their way of looking at the world, assuming that there is only one way of understanding an issue. This could explain why extreme points of view can appear attractive to some autistic people, as they lack the shades of grey that characterise modern thought. However, recent research indicates that some autistic people can over-empathise, soaking up the emotions of others, but have difficulty processing those emotions, leaving them overwhelmed. Autism is becoming better understood as a 'double empathy' problem as it's as much about neurotypical folk thinking differently to autistic people as the other way around.

Language difficulties

Among autistic people, the ability to communicate with language will vary enormously. Some parents have experienced their children developing language, only then to see them gradually and irreversibly lose the power of speech. Some may have a limited vocabulary of no more than twenty or thirty words. Delays in reading and writing can limit the development of speech and general communication.

Echolalia

Some autistic people have echolalia: they repeat phrases or words. This can be a normal part of speech acquisition, but can sometimes show arrested development. I know someone who has a child who would repeat phrases that amused him, even if they were not relevant. One example of this was saying, 'That's a safety violation' in many inappropriate contexts.

One keen primary schoolchild might hear the phrase, 'positive mindset' in an assembly and repeat it to a parent to the point of irritation! A younger child mimic could copy radio jingles and shout the names of DJs, the jingles being easy for them to remember.

The triad of impairments

At the root of all of this is the 'triad of impairments' that people on the autistic spectrum show, a concept which comes from the work of Lorna Wing and Judith Gould.[7] As stated earlier, the three main aspects of life with which autistic people have difficulties are: social interaction, communication and imagination. Some people are arguing for this to be reduced to two, as the second and third features seem to overlap sufficiently to mean that it would make more sense to see them as one. Wing and Gould saw impaired social interaction as a consequence of differences in social communication and social imagination.

1. *Social interaction problems* for autistic people include reading the emotions of others (and themselves), and understanding social 'cues'. These might be shown by selective mutism, where the person cannot or will not speak in certain situations. There will be difficulty in developing enough consideration of the needs of others. They can feel vulnerable and exposed in situations where others feel comfortable. Relationships with others can be complicated. People on the autistic spectrum can be unable to take turns as they may not understand why they should wait.
2. *Social communication* We may need either to change the way we communicate or be prepared to explain the way we speak much more often than we would normally expect. Many

people with autism take spoken messages literally. Autistic people might have difficulty in understanding idioms such as 'raining cats and dogs'. Phrases like 'Hang on a minute' will potentially make them anxious when a minute passes but the action promised does not happen. Euphemisms, jokes and use of other languages may be beyond understanding.

Remember that as we cross into other languages, there are many idioms that seem strange to us. Many autistic people will find the use of irony or sarcasm really difficult as it does not seem to be plain and straightforward communication, but some kind of game from which they can feel excluded.

We need to be careful what we say and how we say it so that we do not add to a sense of anxiety and unease. We may at first struggle to see why aspects of language use are an issue, but they are for autistic people.

We use language in a number of different ways. These include:

- *Receptive language* – how a person understands language, especially instructions and how we follow stories, films and conversations. Delays here clearly affect the ability to interact with others. Things can be misunderstood and cause distress if we do not try to talk as clearly as possible.

- *Expressive language* is how we use language to communicate with others. Autism either removes language or delays the development of language, which can limit and make communication difficult. One way to support this is narrative therapy, where the person works with a speech therapist to explain and understand a story. This can then be transferred to conversation as they develop.

- Autistic people may find it difficult to sustain *conversation* with others, if they do not take turns or understand the way a conversation is going. They can find it difficult to form relationships with others as a consequence.

3. There can be *social imagination problems.* Autistic people can have difficulty making sense of abstract ideas such as justice or friendship or love. They can find it hard to predict what could happen next in situations or conversations, which neurotypical people have few issues with. This will cause difficulties for autistic people, including some levels of anxiety. There can be issues about discovering the boundary between fantasy and reality. We will need to help people with autism to develop this sense or at least to begin to understand how it works for others. Phrases like 'looking at it from another person's point of view' or 'put yourself in their shoes' are difficult for a person with autism. We will need to be patient as it may be a difficult process to even get a hint of this type of thinking. We also need to try harder to see things from their viewpoint rather than simply trying to impose our own!

Theory of mind

Historically a key to understanding autism was the concept of 'theory of mind' (ToM). This is the idea that we can understand the desires, intentions and beliefs of other people. Typically, this develops in people between the ages of three and five. For autistic people, this is very difficult to do as they have difficulty 'reading' the social cues, hints and body language of typical people. Many believe that autism is marked by acquisition of ToM slowing down or not developing in a way to enable understanding of others. This has the effect of making it difficult to share ideas and feelings or to anticipate what others might think, feel or do. ToM is often tested for by the use of play techniques in order to see how the child uses or moves toys.

Again, recent research indicates autistic people don't have these difficulties when socialising with other autistic people.

Coexisting conditions

As well as the triad of impairments, other co-occurring conditions can be diagnosed. Such conditions can coexist with autism without necessarily being part of it. Examples are listed below.

Anxiety

Anxiety is one thing that many people who are not autistic should actually relate to easily. The characteristics of the condition include irritability, agitation, fear of losing control or fear that something bad is about to happen. Autistic people suffer disproportionately from anxiety. We need to help reduce that anxiety. Anxiety underlines much in the autistic spectrum: we need to realise how crippling anxiety can be.

Sensory processing disorder

Some autistic people also have difficulty managing the sensory information they obtain from touching, hearing or seeing something. This can sometimes lead to what is called 'sensory overload', where one or more of the senses receives too much information at once for the brain to process. The person is overwhelmed by feelings that they find too difficult to control or master. Equally they may seek out sensory stimuli because of this.

Attention deficit hyperactivity disorder (ADHD)

ADHD has become much better known in recent years with celebrities like the broadcaster Richard Bacon and the actor Paddy Constantine making public their diagnoses. The condition can make people act impulsively, with hyperactivity and without the ability to give sustained attention to things. This can be overlapping with other traits, though they can be separate.

Depression

Think for a moment about the different parts of the triad. If you have a life where you find it difficult to communicate, difficult to relate to others and have a different way of thinking, this could lead to mental health issues. Feeling different, feeling that you are isolated will take its toll. We need to give support where we can so that mental health issues such as depression can be avoided.

Pathological demand avoidance

This condition is characterised by trying to avoid the demands being made on you because they cause anxiety. If you avoid choices and actions, you will not have to face change. There is again the issue of anxiety. Children try a number of ways to avoid demands. These can include distraction techniques, singing over voices, shouting, hiding or role play. All of these can be seen or understood as bad behaviour, but we need to be careful before making such a judgement.

Dyslexia

Symptoms of dyslexia include great difficulties in learning to read or spell, in sequencing words or ideas, in planning things accurately and in following complex instructions. Many dyslexics tend to learn with pictures or using different coloured paper or backgrounds to help them understand text. Many autistic people find that pictures are reassuring as they can explain things, but this does not necessarily mean they are also dyslexic.

Dyspraxia

This is a condition that can affect planning, action, language and thought. This may make the person seem clumsy and lack co-ordination in their bodily actions; many autistic people have difficulties with 'executive function' and proprioception which present in a very similar way.

Learning difficulties

Difficulties with learning can range from very severe to very mild. They affect sorting and storing information relating to all kinds of life skills. Difficulty in learning language can be problematic, slowing the understanding of other subjects, as the person takes a longer time to build a vocabulary or is unable to absorb new words.

Phobias

These deep-seated fears may well develop as a consequence of the anxiety people experience. Phobias are irrational, but they can concern everyday events and are very difficult to control. They may be particularly acute in people with autism so we need to show sensitivity here.

Obsessive compulsive disorder (OCD)

This is a disorder characterised by a desire to repeat and check actions such as maintaining safety by locking and unlocking doors. It may be about washing hands several times to remove dirt and therefore the possibility of disease or infection. Tasks are repeated over and over again, as a way to try to stop anxiety. A child might have to check and recheck their electronic bedroom alarm clock so that they can be sure that they are woken by it. The main difference between an autistic person's obsessive interests and OCD is that OCD causes extreme distress, whereas repetitive behaviours for an autistic person generally soothe and reassure them.

Epilepsy

This neurological condition causes interruptions in normal brain functioning, which can cause seizures. These can be particularly acute in autistic people, sometimes with life-threatening consequences.

Hypermobility

The muscles and bones of some people are subject to pains and difficulties due to having different bone and muscle structure from most others. This may make writing or using cutlery difficult. Specialists sell equipment such as knives and forks or writing slopes that can help an autistic child with these problems.

So is this a checklist? No. Autistic children will not have all of these coexisting conditions, but they may have a combination which will make the autism more difficult to manage and deal with for other people. This is where the talk of the spectrum is very useful – not all will suffer from these, and combinations of severity vary too.

Each individual is unique and each person needs to be handled carefully so that as far as possible their needs are met. Stereotyping is not helpful here. The idea of the spectrum or constellation helps us to avoid this and helps ensure that a person receives appropriate and individualised care. The Christian doctrine of each of us being uniquely made in the image of God is one that is important to remember: give every person their dignity. Their uniqueness will include the particular way in which autism manifests itself. This is where autism theory and Christian theology interact.

There are more areas in common between those with autism and others than we think. Take anxiety. Look at the popularity of the writings of Matt Haig in books like *Reasons to Stay Alive* and *Notes from a Nervous Planet.* He has written these about depression and has shown how the current pace of life is producing anxiety at an amazing rate in many of us.

This should make us able to empathise in a way that makes us more understanding of autistic people. We need not always stress differences, but seek to see the common ground: for many, we are much more similar than we might think.

The moments of meltdown – how can these be handled?

Meltdowns are one of the most difficult of autistic behaviours to deal with. They need sensitive handling to avoid further complications. They can feel awkward and embarrassing for the parent/carer at the time and subsequently for the autistic person, who after the event may see the problems they have caused but also during it may be further agitated by the loss of control. The reactions of other people around can be of concern, making the situation even more difficult.

Meltdowns can be triggered by the breaking of a normal pattern, which can cause anxiety to reach an unbearable level. Sensory overload can have the same effect. An autistic person went into a meltdown following attending a fireworks display, as the wait for the fireworks followed by the flashing lights and the loudness of the bangs unsettled them, adding to their anxiety.

Meltdowns don't always seem logical but they have a cause and you will have to address that to help the situation. So in the fireworks incident, the safest thing to do was to remove the person from the noise and the flashing lights so that they might become calm.

I did not really understand about meltdown until today.
So what was it like? A hell.
And I am standing in a park in a town near our home. Screaming.
At my son. Tom has not understood that a visit to the toyshop will not automatically bring him the model he seeks.

'Window shopping' is a concept that does not work with him.

He tried to take the box with the models in to the exit of the shop. I had to snatch it off him and return it to the shelves.

I took him outside and grabbed his hand. He was squirming, angry at the injustice.

'It was what I wanted, Daddy,' he screamed.

'But you don't have the money!' I replied.

But this is not a logical conversation.

A security guard came over.

'Can I help you, sir?'

That was all I needed – the helpfulness of others.

My son continued to struggle.

'It is my son. He is – autistic,' I said desperately.

The man nodded.

'So is my grandson. I understand,' he answers.

I doubted that he did. But I smiled and thought to myself that there are people who have much worse battles than this.

They have them daily, hourly, but still they are able to live with them. Yet what I felt most was embarrassment. And shame.

I grabbed hold of Tom's arm and took him to the park but I was getting angrier. I should be the calm one. The grown-up. But I didn't feel like it.

And then there was that laugh. His laugh. Irritating beyond measure. He did not mean to laugh. It is a nervous reaction and that pained me still further.

I was humiliated and wanted to humiliate in return.

There is a part of me that does not believe that he cannot control this. This is a game, isn't it? He just needed to turn round and say, 'It is just a joke, Daddy.'

But that will not come.

A 'Sorry' was offered but the sniggering that went with it seemed to make it invalid to me.

I screamed, 'When are you going to learn that I am angry, that I am embarrassed by this sort of behaviour? Do you do this at school? No, you do not. Now, don't do it with me.'

He began to go quiet. Something was going in.

'Sorry' was said again, this time with no laughing, no sense however that this is anything beyond trying to avoid sanctions.

I have recited a list of various things which I will take away if he does not do as I ask. Why can't he do as I wish, as I command?

But would any child? Is this his autism or is it just about being an eight-year-old boy with the obsessions that they often have? Was he telling me anything about his condition or just his age?

Eventually, we have come to a park bench. He is now willing to be like an obedient puppy and I tell him to stop there. I go over to a stand and buy a tea. Tea – that will make me calm.

The seller gives me a biscuit and, when I return, I break this in two and give one half to my son.

Tom smiles and says, 'Thanks.'

I sip my tea, now feeling just a little ashamed by the screaming and the way that I have behaved. He lost control, perhaps, but I feel that I have been there too.

The problem of masking

There are other problems that autistic people face. One of these is a technique that is referred to as 'masking'.

All of us at times try to conceal how we are. We say that we are fine when we are not fine, but do not want to have a conversation in which we might reveal how we really feel. Perhaps we do not want to be seen as vulnerable. When we go to a party for example, we may pretend to be more sociable than we actually are.

All people wear masks, we all pretend at times. Some can lie with their face, others cannot. Autistic people can use masking to a radical effect.

Masking is the process where an autistic person attempts to disguise who they are by copying the behaviour of the non-autistic. Some scientists have observed this process developing as early as from about six months old, when autistic babies play with other children and learn to copy ways of speaking or playing. This isn't necessarily a conscious decision. Many studies have argued that the identification of females on the autistic spectrum is delayed compared with males because females are much more able to 'blend in' and hide who they are, and do this innately.

Take, for example, obsessions. You could expect a teenage girl to become a little obsessed about ponies, a pop star or a boy band; knowing the difference between this and what is essentially an autistic trait is not easy. A boy can become obsessive about football or cricket facts – but is that a phase? Or is it hiding in plain sight?

Masking is an attempt to fit in, like the chameleon does in nature, changing colour to merge with its background. Yet ultimately, such behaviour puts a great deal of pressure on the autistic person. They are trying to go against the grain of who and how they are. This makes it difficult to express their true emotions. Trying to suppress what you are thinking and feeling can cause psychological issues. It leads some people to self-harm.

Denying feelings is associated with increased use of drink or drugs to try to control anxiety or depression that can occur as a consequence of trying to hide who someone is.

We need to help, support and encourage the autistic person to come to terms with who they are and move to self-acceptance. Masking will not help. Living as truthfully as possible will, but this is not always easy.

Getting to independence?

Many autistic people may never be able to be truly independent. They may have to accept the care of others in most areas of their lives – feeding, changing and washing for example. However, many on the autism spectrum will be capable of making moves towards being independent. Parents will naturally feel a pull about this. The autistic child who wants to do their homework without support can cause a difficult moment, especially if they have previously had a great deal of help with this task.

We need to encourage moves towards this type of growth, not stifle them. For a Christian, the ideal state is not dependence (except with God) or independence, but it is interdependence, realising that we need each other and that, in the words of John Donne, 'No man is an island.' Pursuing this balance is difficult, but very necessary.

All parents struggle with the increasing independence of their children. Parents of autistic children have to consider safety as well. For example, a child might wish to walk to school alone but lacks the ability to correctly cross roads. There could be a number of ways to handle that situation. Driving the child into school or dropping them off at a safe distance could make the fact that they do not come to school by themselves less of an issue. A gradual approach can be helpful in such situations.

The young autistic person may want to fit in with their peers. Some of their aspirations – such as owning a mobile phone – need to be thought through. The phone could actually help to reduce anxiety as the child will know that they have the potential to ring one of their parents if they are concerned about something, or to be told in advance if their parents will be late collecting them.

We need to think through the steps that can encourage further maturity, while at the same time be aware of the difficulties our autistic children will face. Letting go can be hard for the parent or carer but, if it is encouraged, everyone will benefit.

Diagnosis and beyond

Getting a diagnosis

Many families struggle to get to the point of a formal diagnosis of autism, and need help and support in pursuing this course of action. In the UK Autism Act of 2009, the guidelines for proceeding with a diagnosis are as follows:

- Concerned individuals whether parents, care or support workers can seek advice from their doctor.
- If the GP is concerned, they can make a referral to a specialist. These might include a psychologist, a psychiatrist, a paediatrician and a speech and language therapist to give their wisdom and observations to help progress a diagnosis. It is an evidence-based diagnosis, needing several reports to make a formal process. The next stages follow.
- If the referral takes place after an individual has started to attend school, then an educational psychologist is usually involved, visiting the school setting to observe and gather information from staff. (If a diagnosis has been applied for earlier, they may visit a playgroup setting.)
- If all the professionals agree, then a diagnosis can be made.

The 2009 Autism Act gives a right to a diagnosis for the person involved. This can then help to put in place a plan to make available the care and support needed, in school and other settings.

There have been increasing concerns that many children are being denied formal diagnosis in the UK due to local cutbacks in the health and education services. The process is enormously costly in terms of time and money but it is essential that all governments serve the needs of their citizens. It is something that the church needs to ensure happens so that all have the opportunity to get the help they need to become the people they should be.

In 2017, one health authority was looking at rationing the amount of autism diagnoses it was prepared to acknowledge. A quota system like this cannot be acceptable, as it will mean many families and individuals will be lacking the support they need. It is short-sighted as the health authority might pick up the consequences of this in a number of different ways later on, such as more mental health referral in later life. Short-term economies will certainly lead to long-term misery and costs if applied to this issue.

The trouble with girls . . .

One of the recurring trends of autism diagnosis is the way in which girls are not picked up with the speed that boys are. When I have talked to parents, there are many who are not getting a diagnosis until their daughters are some way into their teenage years. Girls are frequently being wrongly diagnosed as well – with many getting labels for depression when the root of their issues is autism. Society is currently not alert enough to seeing the needs of girls in this area.

Does autism affect girls and boys equally? At the moment, the evidence suggests that boys are much more likely to have autism, but that may reflect the way in which diagnosis is done and the current statistics. New methods of testing might reveal a different picture from the one we think that we have.

The statistics seem to tell us that for every three boys with autism, there is just one girl. My feeling is that there are considerably more autistic females who have yet to be identified.

Professor Francesca Happé, of King's College, London, has suggested that her research shows that at least 300,000 girls and women may be missing from the figures we have on autism, as they have either been misdiagnosed with other conditions or not diagnosed at all.[8]

Research findings are tending to suggest to the experts that there should be more similarity in numbers diagnosed with autism in males and females. Instead of 3:1, it may be closer to parity than we now believe.

What are the reasons for the disproportionately low number of girls diagnosed with autism, as compared with boys?

Historically, many professionals have seen autism as essentially a problem affecting boys. The early research on autism, by Kanner and Asperger, for example, was biased towards examining boys. Boys were more obvious in the way they displayed the condition. There were some girls in the studies but they seem to be marginal to the research undertaken. Some have even talked about autism as being the dysfunction of the male brain, which clearly made it difficult to see it in females.

Carol Povey of the National Autistic Society's Centre for Autism said, 'The problem is that professionals don't understand the different ways autism can manifest in women and girls, with many going through their lives without a diagnosis and an understanding of how they feel different.'[9]

There are many explanations given for this. One argument is that girls are better at masking the markers of the condition. They can be more sociable than boys. Interaction with other girls may help them cope with the environment they are in, but cover the reality of the difficulties they are facing. Or there can be meltdowns and difficulties in forming relationships with their peers, which could be misunderstood as bullying or 'just something that happens to girls.' The passionate interests that a girl can have – in horses, for example – can be viewed as part of adolescence but, as we have seen, they can exist at a level that is intense, which is a marker of autism.

Alternatively, they may be exhibiting symptoms that seem to be linked to other issues such as problems of self-esteem or eating conditions. One study quoted in Carrie Arnold's article, 'The Invisible Link between Autism and Anorexia',[10] suggests that 20 per cent of girls diagnosed with anorexia in fact were showing signs often linked to autism. So even if the eating disorder is dealt with, unless the underlying autism is addressed, these girls are still not getting the care they need.

The markers of autism in a girl may be more subtle than in a boy. So what should we be looking for? Girls may not make the obvious physical movements like stimming (using their body in a series of repetitive actions). The underlying anxiety that many teenagers experience may or may not connect with autism. Girls with autism can be more passive than autistic boys, who might be more assertive and aggressive. Some studies suggest that epilepsy is far more common in girls with autism than boys.

We are now aware of the issues of teenage mental health and anxiety. How much of that concern is really about undiagnosed ASD? We may never know. Yet we really need to know, and urgently.

One of the things we need to do is to argue for more funding, to make sure that the process of helping and supporting girls is as efficient as the one that currently supports boys. We need to challenge the residual mindset that fails to see autism as an issue that affects both sexes and views ASD as just a minor problem for girls. Failure to help autistic females is not acceptable.

The moment of diagnosis

The moment of diagnosis of autism can be a double-edged sword. It can feel like bereavement to a family, as the hopes and dreams that they have entertained for their child seemingly disappear. There may be a very strong emotional reaction, which may not be logical or coherent to begin with. Or it may come as a relief as it explains the differences their child has been experiencing and the parents realise they are not the ones to 'blame' for those.

The prayers and support of a church at this time are vital. Just being a listening ear to those coming to terms with a diagnosis is something we need to encourage people to do. This is every bit as much a transition as leaving home, getting a job, getting married, getting a divorce or having children. It may bring hope. It can lead to fear and confusion, both of which need support.

Imagine it happened to you. How would you react? Who could you call on for help?

Advantages of a diagnosis

While the process of getting a diagnosis can be difficult and stressful, there can be a number of positive consequences. These could include the following:

- *Understanding yourself* – if you are the autistic person. If the person is old enough, this may help them to understand who they are and appreciate the way they think, feel and relate to the world. They may feel less alone, and more able to begin to think about how to navigate the world. I have talked to people who have been diagnosed with ASD as adults. They have said the moment can be traumatic but it can lead to self-acceptance and healing, a realisation that they are of worth and that their 'difference' is not a bad thing, but something to be celebrated.
- Others can have *understanding of the person* they are caring for. When a diagnosis is made, others can begin to treat the person appropriately. Parents, siblings, school, employers or friends can now be supported. This knowledge can mean that they all find ways of behaving and talking that are encouraging and do not add to the autistic person's anxiety.
- It enables the autistic person and/or those who care for them to *obtain the services and supports* that they need. A diagnosis does have power in law and should improve an autistic person's life as a consequence.
- *Relief* – unspoken or difficult-to-describe problems are hard to deal with but once the problem has been identified this can bring a sense of relief. Seeing what the 'problem' is can be the key to transforming the situation. When I was fourteen, my parents realised that I was short-sighted and made sure that I wore glasses. Had some of my problems of

achievement at school before been the product of not being able to see the board? Once the problem had been identified, then it could begin to be addressed. The same is true with autism, with its more profound consequences and effects.

However, there can still be some disbelief at what has been diagnosed. There may be some real fears for the future that will need to be addressed. There is always a process of adjustment to a new situation. This may be long or short, but transition can be difficult.

The bereavement of diagnosis

It may be helpful for some parents to think about the stages of bereavement from the work of Elisabeth Kübler-Ross, who identified what has become known as the 'Five Stages of Grief'[11] when considering responses to a death. This is a good start for us to understand what happens to those in pain and confusion caused by a loss; the diagnosis of autism could be seen as analogous in some ways to the bereavement of a loved one.

The stages are:

1. *Denial.* You cannot believe what has happened and you do your best to try to say that it is not happening.
2. *Anger.* You become angry at the person or others who you think should have supported them. Perhaps you become angry at yourself for not acting or saying something. The anger can be very deep and very emotional.
3. *Bargaining.* Perhaps the situation could be altered if you did something positive. If the autistic person promises to do something, then perhaps they could get better. The person

concerned might see the problem as theirs to fix in some way, when this does not make any sense.

4. *Depression.* You realise that the situation is bad and perhaps you think that there is nothing you can do to change it. You feel powerless and, consequently, you begin to feel depressed. Reality is beginning to be accepted, but that makes the future seem to be something that will be about failure and difficulty. There does not seem to be any hope.

5. *Acceptance.* The process of grieving has begun to incorporate this experience into your life. This is not 'getting over it' or denying its power to shock or unnerve you. This will take time to happen.

Kübler-Ross did not imply that this is a linear process. Bereaved people can go through a variety of different emotions, including these five and others. Several of these emotions will perhaps happen all together which will produce at times an almost unbearable sense of paradox and contradiction. This can overwhelm a person.

When you apply these to the aftermath of a diagnosis of autism, they do make sense of a very difficult and often traumatic experience. The denial may well be quite deep. It may have taken quite a process to get to the diagnosis and the parents might have been quietly convincing themselves that they do not have an autistic child as their youngster does not behave like another child or a stereotypically autistic child.

There may be anger at the comparative slowness to get to the moment of diagnosis. There can be anger at a partner who might have been more sceptical and thus slowed the process of diagnosis. It is not unusual to see antagonism towards a doctor whose diagnosis seems to have given a child a label that the parents perceive to be limiting or damaging in some way.

The bargaining stage can involve the parents refusing to accept what is said and seeking a second opinion, or seeking out those who think they can 'cure' autism. Perhaps they think they can do something to change things. However, they need to come to the point of acceptance to realise that autism is a lifelong condition.

Depression can set in when the diagnosis is made. The time of waiting for diagnosis could well have been a period when a person kept their emotions at bay. At diagnosis the reality hits them; they may find themselves overwhelmed by what they believe to be the consequences of autism.

Reflection – accepting the reality of autism

The move to acceptance will take a while. Indeed, for some it may be a process that never ends, just as the bereavement of a loved one can never truly reach the 'getting over it' stage. What parents need here is the support and the encouragement of friends, and possibly more formal counselling to help them to adjust to the new reality.

This is a point where the church needs to model supportive love, to live out the words of Paul in Galatians 6:2: 'Help to carry one another's burdens, and in this way you will obey the law of Christ' (gnb). It is important that Christian friends share the experience of those involved in a diagnosis of ASD, and encouragement at this time is vital.

The process of diagnosis can take people to dark places. We need to be there with them. We cannot offer them Easter Sunday joy while they are feeling the sadness and the desolation of Easter Saturday. There can be darkness, a depression which we must not ignore, and through which we take care to offer help.

Supporting people through this difficult and confusing time will be a challenge. If we are the people doing this, we may hear things that will shock us and seem out of character for the parents dealing with the diagnosis. There is a need to be sensitive; giving support and trying to encourage the way forward, while not denying the darkness they may well feel.

Prayer

Dear Father, help all of those involved in the support of people with autism and their families to have love, patience, understanding and grace. Give them wisdom in what to say and how to support, to be good listeners and to see the value of all people.

Amen

Part Two

The Difficulties the Autistic Person Faces

3

At Home

Autism presents in very different ways, but it is not a sliding scale. The spectrum or constellation idea is an important one to remember – no two children are the same. When you are told that your child is on that spectrum, the fine points of this are lost. You could have a sense of bereavement at the loss of the child you had anticipated, knowing that this child has a disability.

Then bureaucracy creeps in. In order to get the support you need, you might need to fill in unbelievably long forms, where you have to explain what your child can and cannot do, an experience which can be demoralising.

It is important to remember that when the diagnosis is given it is not possible to predict how the person may develop. With support and love, some autistic children will end up being barely noticeably different to their peers. For some others it will be obvious, who may show it by being unable to have well-developed relationships with their peers.

As a parent, I have made the following observations.

An autistic child can become very frustrated

Frustration is sometimes due to a lack of the ability to communicate, which can lead to anger and mood swings. As a parent, you can reinforce this pattern if you are not careful. Patience isn't just a virtue or one of the fruits of the Spirit – it becomes a necessary part of a toolbox to help you as a parent deal with some of the difficult situations you may encounter. It is important to think ahead about how to deal with them. As parents, we are guarding against our own sense of fatigue and our limited ability to cope with the situations we face. We will need to have inner reserves – so self-care is important, as is the support of others of your role as parent.

An autistic child's need for set patterns and how this might affect a family

One autistic child becomes uneasy if, for example, she cannot view certain television programmes at the time she thinks she should be watching them. Although she understands the principle of digital recorders or playback facilities and such machines, the need to do some things at certain times is very important to her. I have reflected that in the 1970s, with no way of recording or replaying programmes, this must have led to distress. Or is it that our technology is contributing to this issue as we can watch and re-watch almost anything? Our culture of instant access could be both a blessing and a curse.

Anxiety

No parent wants their child to be anxious or worried. Anxiety is a much heightened experience for a person on the autistic spectrum. Avoiding saying things or behaving in ways that increase the child's personal anxiety can be very difficult. The anxiety can be about a past event, which the autistic child feels colours all other events, even those that have no direct connection to it. Anxiety might express itself by the child wanting to hold on to a toy or an object. He might pinch his own skin or do other self-harming things in order to help relieve the pressure. Parents need to keep a watchful eye open for such behaviour.

It was one of the great ironies of 2017 that an item invented to help manage anxiety became a craze. The fidget spinner and the fidget cube were designed to help people with autism deal with their anxiety, not to be toys for all children. I know of schools where these items were banned, despite the fact that before the craze autistic children had used them successfully. Parents of an autistic child need to help find objects he can use to calm himself.

Be clear about expectations

Where is the boundary between behaviour linked to autism, and deliberately bad behaviour? This is a really difficult question. Children are not perfect but we should be careful to make sure we do not discipline them unnecessarily harshly.

If you need to punish behaviour, be very careful about how you express the way you will punish. If you make an idle threat, and then sort out the situation without carrying out your threat, the child will not realise the punishment is not to be enforced. For example, after his autistic son had been particularly bad, a father banned him from seeing a specific television show. A few weeks later, the father asked why his son was not watching that show, and was told it was because the father had banned him from doing so! If you change your mind – especially if you had said something only in the heat of the moment – make sure that you are clear about things.

Be clear and reassure, always explain, and then check until you are sure that all the messages have been understood.

Encouragement

Your autistic daughter might not succeed in the ways you expect. Where there is success, it is important to celebrate and affirm her. (This is true of every child but especially of an autistic child.) It is vital to help children develop a sense of their own worth. Let us face it – encouragement is manure to the soul that we could all be spreading more liberally!

Dislikes

Be aware that there are things that some autistic people do not like. They may well have difficulty with some textures of materials or foods. They might have a hypersensitivity to light or noise. They might be more acutely aware of certain noises that cause distress. It is important that those caring for them learn these dislikes and reduce the possibility of encountering a sensory overload that could greatly distress the person with autism.

Be careful when booking tickets, as the more immersive forms of cinema such as 3D or 4DX (which use effects such as rocking the seat or spraying with water) could cause a sensory meltdown as the element of uncertainty and shock might be very distressing.

Possibilities

All children can surprise us. Be prepared to accept and seek to understand, to comfort and affirm. This can be hard as a family – 'Why aren't we allowed to do such things?' Yet this is where, from a Christian point of view, we need to be demonstrating the agape love that Jesus showed to us.

There is an essential paradox deep at the heart of parenting that having an autistic child can magnify. In a sense, all parenting is about teaching the child to become independent of the parent, to create autonomy in the child. Now, this presents the Christian parent in particular with a dilemma. We should be seeking to model the love of God, where we are encouraged to become more dependent on the Father, the perfect God. We need to let our children go, to let them become more independent of us and, from a spiritual point of view, more dependent for themselves on God.

The need to support siblings and other relatives

How do we help relatives and others deal with the reality of autism? They will need guidance and support. If you can, help them to feel that they can say what they need to say, however initially shocking that might sound to others.

Some older relatives, such as grandparents, may not understand the concept of autism, or may dismiss signs of it as an ordinary developmental stage in the child's life. They will have notions of 'normal', which can be described as neurotypical. We need to make sure that we give them all the idea that it does not have to be a tragedy if one child does not fulfil their expectations. The diagnosis of autism is likely to have come as a shock to them, and we need to realise they need time to adapt. People may struggle to own what they are seeing.

Brothers and sisters may well find their autistic sibling very difficult to live with. They may not see their autistic relative as 'normal' and feel sad about this. What does a child mean by 'normal' in this context? What is making them sad? Children are much more openly conformist than their parents, who might try to disguise their own sadness. We need to take the difficulty of having an autistic sibling seriously; otherwise we may end up giving our other children problems.

It takes time to adjust to the idea that someone you know and love is autistic. Having someone in the house who is autistic can be difficult for some children to handle, especially if the autistic child's behaviour includes meltdowns or mood swings.

As we have already seen, for a parent, there can be a sense of bereavement, and so too for the siblings. We need to make sure we are listening to them, and understanding their feelings. Sometimes they can feel that they are expected to be an unpaid carer for their autistic brother or sister. As parents, we need to value them and give them good quality time with us, just as we do for their sibling. They need attention, and not to feel that their autistic sibling is more important than they are. This is very difficult, especially where the input needs to be greater the more severe the needs of the autistic child.

The younger members of the family may well need help and support, through siblings groups or specialised counselling. We need to encourage them to have relationships with peers who can help them. Interacting with other children will give the sibling a chance to see the boundaries of play and acceptable behaviour as these might well have been tested or re-defined by their experience with their brother or sister.

Many local authorities have siblings groups, where the brothers and sisters of autistic children or children with other conditions can all meet together so that they can have a safe space to talk about their experiences with those who most understand what they are going through. These groups provide social activities such as picnics, cooking, games nights and other opportunities. They are led by trained youth workers who can give support to siblings.

Adults offering sympathy or guidance are important. So too are people of a similar age who have lived the issue, who can refer to events and reflections they have made about the problems of having an autistic sibling.

It is worth making sure that the school that the non-autistic sibling goes to knows about their sibling's condition, in case the stresses of living in such an environment ever become a difficulty that spills over into school.

Creating the right conditions for autistic people in our homes

The houses we live in become homes when we adapt them to our needs and the style of family life with which we feel comfortable. This is about making them places where we can escape the anxiety or the stress of the outside world, where we can be ourselves. Yet for autistic people, even the home can be a place where stress and anxiety can be part of their daily experience.

Tara Leniston and Rhian Grounds, in their book *Coming Home to Autism*,[1] set out to approach dealing with your child's diagnosis and the necessary changes you could consider making to a home as a consequence. They look at all the key rooms in a house, including the bedroom, kitchen, sitting room, the toilet and the garden. They raise questions and give suggestions in order to help the child be safe and not overwhelmed in their own house. It is a very thoughtful and sensible book, which gives some good advice and practical solutions to issues families face.

You can do an audit of your home. Look at each room to assess each area where there might be issues for an autistic child. Talk to a family or a person with more experience, to help you examine issues that will make life at home more difficult than it needs to be.

Parental difficulties in caring for an autistic person

It is not easy being the parent of an autistic child. If we expect perfection then we will be sadly disappointed in all our children! We need to be honest about who we are and how we function. All of us have times when we get impatient or feel frustrated. Being the parent of an autistic child can be a flash point. Their behaviour in public can make us feel vulnerable to the remarks of others, especially if we feel that we have failed to behave in a mature way in a difficult situation. We might feel embarrassed or angry.

Simon was finding it increasingly difficult to deal with Tom. One Sunday, the family left their church and went to one nearby. A day off for a vicar is often a day to evaluate the opposition. This was going to be a family service. To Simon's mind, this meant it would be short. Short was good as it meant that it could connect with Tom. But it became a moment of agony. Well, nearly an hour of it.

Tom seemed to make random noises all the way through the service. Then he started sticking his tongue out during the hymns, as if he were a lizard about to catch a fly.

'Tom – put your tongue back in – now! Did you hear me? Do it, now!' Simon was on the edge of shouting at him.

'Need the toilet,' said Tom.

Tom used needing the toilet as a way to deflect tension, Simon thought. Whether Tom actually thought about what he was doing, though, was difficult to be sure about. But Simon was grateful for this break from the service.

'I'll take him,' he told Carol. 'You stay here and enjoy the service.'

Carol smiled. A rest even for a few minutes was welcome even if the family service they were in was particularly grim and not what she had expected. Just not having to worry about what Tom would do next was a relief. When they got to the toilet in the church hall, Tom seemed distracted and missed the bowl. Simon didn't say anything but got the toilet paper and mopped up, before telling his son to pull his trousers up. Why couldn't Tom just concentrate and get it in the bowl?

Was this going to be how it was for the rest of his life? Telling his son off? Telling him the simplest instructions several times? Simon sighed to himself.

But that was how it was going to be – okay, so be it. He had to find some patience in all this, didn't he? It would come. He was sure that some grace might help him.

Resignation is not the best quality in a parent. It takes the place of love, real love and caring.

But at least it was not despair. That was Simon's ever-present temptation, though.

Making sure we obtain what our children need

The pursuit of justice is an important Christian virtue. Micah reminds us to seek justice as part of following the Lord. We often seem so keen on stressing love that we mistake this love for a sentiment which does not affirm that ways of thinking and living need challenging too.

We need to abandon passivity and try to be assertive. We are speaking on behalf of others but we need to make sure that their human rights and our needs are protected. We cannot afford to be passive when it comes to these areas. We can politely but firmly seek justice and support. Jesus did not reject the Syro-Phoenician woman when she was a little forward, or the woman with bleeding when she touched him in the middle of the crowd. Both of these women spoke up and they were helped. We must make sure that we share our experiences with others so that they can avoid some of the problems we have had to face.

It is vital that the church gives parents support at the time of diagnosis, as the thought that your child may never be able to do even seemingly simple tasks, like tying their own shoelaces, can seem overwhelming. However, we also need to realise that we are taking a snapshot of what is happening and it does not have to be this way forever. With support, children can achieve more than we might feel they can. We will need to be their advocates when others don't share our faith in them.

The filling-in of forms

There are benefits in the UK which are related to disability. These include payments to help the disabled person directly, as well as money to help support the designated carer of the person so that they can have money that might decrease their need to work in order to offer more extensive support. Yet to apply for these benefits a bureaucratic process has to be undertaken.

If we are going to be a carer, then we need to make sure that we get what we are entitled to for the care of the child. In the UK, there are two sources of funding that can help families in this respect. There is, first, Carer's Allowance, which provides a monthly benefit for those who are looking after people with needs. There is, second, Disability Living Allowance, which provides money to help with the child.

Unfortunately, these come to us via a bureaucracy that seeks to check in detail what our children can and cannot do. In the television series, *The A Word*, the character Eddy asked why was it necessary for Joe – the autistic child – to be able to hop, a question from one of the forms. I don't know many adults that hop regularly – is it an essential skill?

I have known parents who have felt that they would rather not fill in the form. However, it is needed. Is the bureaucracy not wise to the extra distress? The answer is that it probably isn't and we need to communicate that to them, to make them realise that there are human, feeling people at the end of their forms. However, there is a need to give an accurate picture of what the autistic person needs, to receive the appropriate support.

A parent or carer filling in the form will probably be facing again the starkness of what their child can or cannot do. Coming face to face with the cataloguing of things their child can or cannot do is powerful and disturbing. The task triggers in some people a more profound sense of loss than even the original diagnosis. They will need to be encouraged to realise that the form is a snapshot of a moment but not necessarily a permanent truth. Give them your support and help them to find peace with what is a difficult process.

We need to encourage each other that our children are not lists of failures or successes – they are people, with potential.

When do we name autism to children?

Telling parents and friends that your child has a disability is very difficult, especially if the child does not obviously 'look' disabled, as is true of many people on the autistic spectrum. There is an even more difficult conversation to be had, which many parents may well dread.

One of the issues that came up in the first episode of Series Two of *The A Word* is when parents and children should have the conversation about the word 'autism'. Joe mentioned it in the programme before his parents – did he see it as a bad thing? Is there just one moment or is it a series of moments when you have the conversation about what autism means and what it means to be a person with autism?

The word cannot be avoided and the longer the parent puts off the discussion with a child who is becoming self-aware, the more difficult the outcome. Not all autistic people will have the conversation, as they may be non-verbal, but those who are verbal need to address this.

Talking about the word can be liberating for some, as the autistic person may then be more able to make sense of why they feel or think as they do. We need to make sure that we do not limit them with a label. Descriptions do not have to become entrapping or imprisoning if they are handled properly. Autistic people can take a certain pride or confidence in their identity. However, we need to make sure that we do not end up making them feel superior. We need to give them a rounded view of who they are and what they might achieve. Explaining the idea of the spectrum, and that each person will have unique attributes or issues, is an important way in which to help an autistic person develop an appropriate and realistic self-image.

For many, having the label can actually bring a feeling of release. They are able to identify with the descriptions of what autism is, and can say, 'That's me!'

The trouble with normal . . .

One of the worst parts of parenting is the seeming competitiveness that parents can get involved in, where their children are measured against other people's progress or development. When one of your child's peers hits a milestone, such as their first steps or their first words, this can be a difficult moment for parents with autistic children, for whom that stage may be reached comparatively very late or not at all.

The Canadian songwriter Bruce Cockburn has a song called *The Trouble with Normal*, which is about what is acceptable politically, but it has a power for us too. 'Normal' can be quite an oppressive word if used wrongly as some kind of power statement against which we measure people and their 'achievement'.

Tom's parents tried to ignore all pressure to conform but it never seemed to be likely that Tom would achieve so-called normal life. But there was a problem with normal – it meant conformity, being just like other people, didn't it? That was the way that Simon tried to reason this out once. The best thing was to be who you were, and then to embrace allowing Tom to be Tom. A fine theory, but the reality was less than that. Simon and Carol were determined to try and bring some hope to Tom.

As he grew, Tom would sit on his chair at meal times. He would seem to simply stare at the wall. There did not seem to be any life there. There was blankness. He would not even look at his food unless his parents cajoled him.

Simon could not understand why his son behaved like this and would try to use words to encourage Tom to concentrate. Tom looked but did the little boy ever see anything? What was the beyond that he seemed to be staring at? A part of Simon would have liked to have made this some telling spiritual strength – that his son was staring beyond earth to some heavenly place. Yet the truth was he was just – staring. Often Simon would put his hand in front of Tom's face to try to stop him from becoming fixated on the wall. But Tom did not seem to flinch. He simply moved his head away from the hand. There were no laughs, no sense of a child playing 'Peepo' as many infants play. Would he ever respond?

'Why are you staring, Tom?' Simon asked. There was nothing, absolutely nothing to look at.

'Why, Daddy?' echoed Tom. The little boy continued to stare at the wall and his eyes did not flicker with any sense of recognition at anything his father was saying.

'Yes – why?' Simon felt the blood rushing into his face and he wanted to slam his fist on to the table to get a reaction. But he knew that did not make any sense and he felt the restraining idea almost like a pair of invisible handcuffs.

'Why?' came back the question. 'Why, Daddy?'

'Answer me!' Simon was getting more frustrated. He wanted his son to speak to him, to give him a sentence, not an echo.

'Answer me,' parroted Tom. 'Answer me.'

Simon put his head in his hands and began to cry. As he sat there by his son, he felt a little hand on his shoulder.

A voice said, 'Daddy.' Tom repeated the word several times.

In his head, Simon heard this as 'Daddy, don't cry.' He just wished that was what his son had said, rather than just 'Daddy'. There was someone in there; there was a person; he felt this showed it. But one imprisoned by his condition.

Didn't Tom realise the frustration that his autism was giving to his parents? One part of Simon hoped that his son never did. If Tom ever understood, that would be a sadness that would seem unbearable. Better for him to remain ignorant of the pain.

That way he might be able to retain some chance of a childhood.

Socialising

Two weeks before the party, Carol found she was losing sleep and this ended with nights of continuous insomnia. She did not admit this to Simon to begin with but, after three nights, she was feeling fragile.

Simon was eating his breakfast one morning in the kitchen when she said, 'I need to talk to you. It's Tom's birthday party.' She looked as if she were about to cry.

Simon sighed inside with relief and hoped that this had not become external – it had not.

'His birthday?' This seemed to him to be quite a way off and not in need of a discussion at this hour of the day.

'Yes. I'm worried.'

What had she to be worried about? 'Why?' Carol clearly thought it was obvious that he should share her worry about whatever-it-was but he just could not see what was upsetting her.

'I'm not sure that anyone will want to come.' She sounded serious.

Simon put his bowl down and looked at her. 'You're not sure anyone will come?'

'That's what I said.' Did he ever really listen to what she was saying?

Simon could tell that she was angry with him for echoing what she said. She believed that he was being patronising. Simon thought that he was showing real care by showing he was listening to her words.

'Are you actually listening to me at all, Simon? I am worried sick that none of the people in Tom's class will come to his birthday party.'

Simon looked at her. 'Have we actually invited anyone yet?'

'No,' she sighed.

'How can you say that? If you have not invited anyone, then no one can reject you, can they?' Simon thought he was being logical. Why didn't she listen to him? He was getting frustrated with her. He was being logical.

He was being stupid, Carol thought. 'Look, I'm worried that when I do give out the invitations, they won't come to the party because of Tom's autism. They might not want to play with the weird kid. They will find excuses and that will hurt him.'

Carol thought that she was saying what had to be said, but Simon hated it when she chose to use such stark language about his son. He could take it from professionals, but he wanted to perhaps hide a little within his own mind by making sure that when they were together, they said only positive things about Tom to make sure that Simon could feel better.

'I am sure that the kids in his class will come. They don't really think of Tom as the weird kid – they are too young to think in those terms. And I have never known a parent tell me that their child has avoided a party as the birthday boy or girl has a disability.'

Carol sighed and then said, 'They are hardly likely to tell you, Simon, are they? I mean, this isn't something that you want to talk about but I am sure that it happens and it could happen to our son. I mean, it is up there with racism as something that nice middle-class women will do. I don't want him to be hurt if they decide not to come.' Carol had a certainty in what she was saying that unnerved

Simon. As though she had already decided that there was going to be a major problem.

'Are you sure that this is about Tom or is it about how you feel about him?' He tried to move things on, 'Look, why don't we start writing and giving out the invitations? Then we can see if there really is a problem or not.'

She grimaced and replied: '"It is a worry in your silly little head, dear?" Is that what you were going to say, Simon? Because if you were, I am quite in the mood for screaming the house down and making a big scene so I hope you weren't about to say that! I am sick to death of the fact that you don't take seriously what is happening to us. When are you going to care, Simon? When?'

'I care, I really care,' he said.

For the next few days, they were concerned about how to give invitations out and they still had the lingering doubt about whether or not there would be guests. Slowly, those invited acknowledged. Ten boys from Tom's class said they were coming. Ten boys – it seemed like a miracle!

This was a moment when Simon began to feel that Carol's fears had been misplaced and that there was going to be a hopefully good birthday party where everyone, and especially Tom, would feel good at the end of the process. This did not stop Carol from worrying.

When the day arrived for the birthday party, the children all came, feeling excited. They were all eager to play and have a good time. It was a party, after all.

One of them – was it David? – said to Simon, 'We like Tom. He's different but we like him.'

Simon was not sure whether he should be proud or depressed by this – oddly, he seemed to feel both at the same time.

The boys began to sing 'Happy Birthday, Tom' when the cake came out. Tom began to join in. He was seemingly unaware of himself. His parents looked at him and, slowly, Tom began to sense their disapproval. *Gradually, he sang more quietly, stopping before the end of the song.*

The cake was cut. The goodie bags were given out, after everyone had survived all the tiring games – the hit the donkey, the blind man's bluff, the variant of twister. There were loud laughs all the way through the afternoon and, even when it began to rain, they did not get disheartened.

The next day, David's mum saw Carol. She told her how much her son had enjoyed the party. Perhaps she could try another one next year?

Socialising our children

All parents can become concerned about the ability of their child to make friends. Birthday parties can be very difficult, as they reveal the fault lines in an autistic child's ability to get on with others. Similarly, many parents are rightly concerned about the social progress their child with autism may or may not be making at school. This is particularly true while the child is at primary school, where there is a large emphasis on the social aspects of education.

Every parent wants their child to have friends. Perhaps this is because we don't want them to be alone. Maybe we are aware of a time when we might not be there, so they could need support from other people. Possibly it is because we know that we are unlikely to be there for all of their lives and we want them to be cared for. Making friends will be a struggle for some children. It may not happen, or certainly not in the way we expect.

We have to learn that we cannot make children become friends with anyone. Friendships are choices that they make and we are likely to have little if any influence on them. We need to realise that some children – both autistic and non-autistic – make friends at different speeds. Putting them under any pressure will heighten their anxiety and their sense of isolation.

The level at which we perceive friendships can sometimes be problematic. All of our friends probably started as acquaintances and the relationships deepened to friendships over a period of time. We need to encourage relationships, but we need to not put unrealistic stress on them. Let them grow organically.

Think for a moment about how much anxiety relationships have caused us. Then consider how much more difficulty that causes those who are already experiencing anxiety daily as part of their autism.

If we show tension or worry about friendships to our autistic children, all we are likely to do is increase their anxiety and confusion about this process. We need to allow them the time to develop relationships, and not to worry if they do not fit with the perceived pattern we think makes sense.

Dealing with frustration

Many of those who live with autistic people find that they feel frustration. This is to be expected but it is a difficult emotion to confront in ourselves. When there is repetitive or challenging behaviour, then there can be the sense of 'why can't they be reasonable?'

Many parents will find the level of frustration difficult to cope with. For the sake of their own mental health, they may need to seek out support so that they can have the networks they need.

We need to be particularly aware that we can sometimes find ourselves losing our tempers and behaving inappropriately. It is unacceptable to smack children nowadays. Even getting annoyed with a disabled child because of some behaviour of theirs that isn't naughty or challenging is unwarranted. But it is a temptation that may grow from frustration. We will need grace to deal with this – a grace based in love.

Helping to develop motor skills

One of the great problems for parents who have an autistic child lies in the area of motor skills. Holding cutlery, riding a bike and catching a ball can all seem very slow to develop, if at all. Holding a pen might well hurt some autistic children; being encouraged to use a sloped writing surface helps some of them. Thought and care are needed. Don't rush the child. Allow them to make small victories and they may well end up succeeding more than if they are forced to try to achieve too much too soon.

There are companies who specialise in producing cutlery and other items that are adapted for the needs of people who have hypermobility or sensory sensitivity. Their specially de-signed products can be found online.

If you are in a relationship

Dealing with autism can be a very difficult load to bear. What is essential is that, if you are married, then you and your part-ner help and support each other. You need to make sure that the relationship has good roots. Take care to talk to each other about your emotions concerning the situation.

As we have seen, the process of diagnosis can be traumatic for many. The adjustment to the concept of having a child with a disability can be equally profound. The work of bringing children up is hard, but it can be doubly so if you are trying to deal with a condition like autism with its unknown difficulties. Although we commit in marriage to being there when life gets difficult, it is particularly hard to face the reality of the challenging situations autism sometimes brings.

Your marriage matters not just for you and your partner. I recently talked to an autistic person whose mum and dad had split up after his diagnosis. Rightly or wrongly, he saw this as the reason why their relationship fell apart. It was probably not that straightforward – but imagine the guilt that the person carries if he thinks it is. We need to stay strong for each other and for our children: this is not easy and may require much prayer.

All good parenting is a long battle with our own selfishness and putting the needs of our children before our own, which can be difficult within any family set-up. When we are facing living with a child with a disability, we need to make sure that we are honest with each other and giving the support we will need.

Make sure too that you don't hide yourself in your career or a role outside of the family to avoid facing the responsibilities. If God has blessed you with children, your first spiritual role is to look after and encourage them; anything else in the community, in your workplace and in church is of secondary importance.

If there are grandparents who are of an age and with an understanding, encourage them to support you. If your autistic child does not have that blessing, do not be afraid of going to your church family.

If we know parents who are bringing up an autistic child by themselves, we need to make sure that we are supporting them in practical and loving ways. A spiritual 'mum' or 'dad' could be valuable here, giving support and encouragement when most needed.

Reflection: the power of words

From a Christian point of view, words should not always frighten us. God spoke and the universe came into being. The Word became flesh and salvation happened. As James rightly points out, the tongue can be used to build up or destroy. Naming autism may well reinforce negatives, but it does not have to be like that. It may bring both child and parents freedom as they learn to accept the reality they live in. 'The truth will set you free,' Jesus told his disciples. Handled well, facing this difficult conversation can be the beginning of a better life, not a lesser one.

Prayer

Father, when the time comes to name autism, help us to be truthful, encouraging and loving. Let the moment be about possibility not limitations, a moving on and not a moving back.

Father, help us to pursue justice, so that all those who need support for their autism receive the help they need. Help us to keep going if we are parents. Help us to support if we are friends or family. Let those in authority never forget their responsibilities to the most vulnerable.

Amen

4

Education

Preschool

Think back to a moment when you first went to school or university or a new job. How scared were you? How excited? Did you have both feelings at the same time? Recall these as you think about the role of education in the life of an autistic person. This challenge is why we need to prepare for education and its demands.

The earlier the intervention for the autistic child, the better the long-term outcomes can be. In the UK, trained professionals can visit preschool children to help with their understanding of language and their social communication skills. Speech therapy can be offered to children before they start at school, which can enable them to begin to make progress.

We need to ensure that playgroups and nursery schools are prepared to work with children of different needs. There are some that seek to specialise in caring for children with special needs, so parents will need to consider whether the best thing for their child is to follow that path or for them to seek out a more traditional group which will help the child. Playgroups are centred on the need for communication and social interaction, so their staff should soon spot issues.

Adjustments: going to school

Transitions are always difficult and we need to be aware of these. Preparing for going to school is one of the most important points of transition and so we need to make sure that we get this right for an autistic child. All people find the transitions from playgroup or home to school difficult in some way. We will need to make sure there is careful thought and planning to reduce the anxiety. An official education and health care plan will not usually be in place by the time the autistic child first goes to primary school. It is important that school and parents pursue one as early as possible if the child's needs require one and, even without one, make reasonable adjustments to help the child. The use of a visual timetable to show the order of the day will help to reduce anxiety as the pattern is seen and talked through with the child.

Progressing to secondary school can be an even bigger issue. Many secondary schools will offer an experience of the school before the child is due to move there. As well as the introduction to the building via the parents' information in the autumn before moving, there should be opportunities for the child to visit the building during the day, such as being aware of issues like bells and moving from one classroom to another.

Tom started school when he was nearly five years old. Carol and Simon had managed to get him on the special needs register and were working for a statement to be put in place.

There was a seemingly endless series of meetings in which Tom was assessed, measured against a checklist, and given targets that would help him to succeed. Thankfully, he had not lost his words as some autistic children do but he was just very slow in acquiring language. Neither did he hit out at other children. There were rages but these were at home, where Carol had to cope with them as they often happened around bedtime and Simon was always at some church meeting.

Supports for autistic people

Visual triggers are often helpful to autistic children. For example, students can be given a visual timetable, showing periods for each weekday, with different symbols and colours linked to the subjects being studied. A photo-book showing them key teachers and rooms will also help prepare them for the changes they will encounter. (These aids can also be of use to autistic adults when preparing to go to college or a new job.)

Some autistic people will have particular needs that will require special consideration in the following areas.

1. Some students might have a special *sensitivity to sound*. In some situations, ear defenders can help with relaxation. They have the effect of reducing the large sounds and enable attention. Cinemas for children sometimes have an 'autism-friendly' performance, where the sound is turned down and people are allowed to come and go as they please.

2. *Interactions with others*. Although education involves socialisation, some students can be given permission to work near the teacher. They need to be somewhat isolated as this will make them feel much more relaxed. Others need to make sure that there are times when they can withdraw totally from the need to socialise so that they feel less anxious about the pressures this can cause.

3. *Interaction with others and behaviour*. It may be that other students think that an autistic student is 'looking at them funny'. Similarly an autistic student may have this concern. It is important to make sure that this does not lead to growing conflict.

4. *The presence of other people* such as learning assistants will enable an autistic student to share their concerns with a trusted adult once a relationship is established. This is desirable, so that any anxieties can be addressed quickly.

5. *Clear instructions.* Although clarity is helpful to all students it is especially so for those on the autistic spectrum, as they need to guard against the anxiety they may feel if they are not sure about a task. Patience can be shown either by repeating the instructions, or better still by having them written on a piece of paper or the board for the child to access them.

6. *Allowing a student not to take part in a drama or role-play.* While these are good techniques to help students learn, they can be quite difficult for some autistic students who lack social imagination. They may find role-play difficult, and expressing emotions might be troublesome, especially if some of these are extreme. The freer nature of group work and possible noise can induce anxiety. That said there are some autistic students who love drama and role-play – it's important to know the individual.

7. I have found it necessary to *talk to autistic students one at a time*, away from a group, to reassure them. Occasionally I may make them aware of social norms so that they do not cause unnecessary stress for themselves. They should never be singled out within a group.

8. It is important to me as a teacher to *check the information the Special Education Needs (SEN) department gives* me so that I do not start teaching an autistic child while assuming they are like any other child. SEN departments are good at handling and passing on quite precise instructions about how to handle autistic children as they have good links with primary feeder schools and with agencies that have been working with a student.

9. Talking with parents at *parents' evenings* has been invaluable as it has made me aware of their problems. I have tried to make appropriate changes in my classroom to maximise their children's learning experiences. Parents are the experts on their child's condition, and can help teachers avoid putting the child in a difficult situation.

10. It is important to *prepare autistic students for any change* – a new seating plan, the absence of a member of staff, or a change of group – well in advance, if possible, to avoid undue anxiety.

11. *It is important to listen.* If a child has a particular interest, some time should be given to listening to that, to show that they are valued, and related to as a person. This will help develop their sense of self-worth.

12. Allow an autistic student *time away from a particularly noisy lesson*, so that it does not disturb them.

13. Some schools allow an autistic student to *leave classrooms a little early* so they can make their way out through the corridors without the noise and bustle of changeover times.

14. Some schools allow an autistic student to *miss the last period of the day*, going and finding a designated SEN teacher or support worker so that the student can unwind. Think about the pressure of trying to concentrate all day if you find that difficult. Afternoon lessons are often really challenging to autistic children who have tried all morning to keep working. Homework concerns may need to be addressed, as may any negative interactions.

15. *Use electronic communication wisely.* Most schools now have internet sites to inform parents. Homework sites can include websites, worksheets and other information for students. Children can tick off items on homework lists when they have completed them. This reduces stress as a child will know when and where homework is to be delivered. However, some teachers will forget or put the wrong date on homework, so double-check by email if there is any sign of anxiety about this for the child.

16. How does the school deal with *bullying that can be linked to the autistic student*? There must be a good system in place to support and remove any such problems.

How can schools and parents work together?

Many schools practise a phased move from playgroup to school, gradually building up the number of hours a child does over a number of weeks. They will do home visits or meet with the parents to discuss ways forward.

It may be that by the time your child reaches school, a great deal of the documentation that indicates your child's needs has reached the staff there. If there has not been a move in the direction of a diagnosis, begin to work with the school as soon as possible to make sure that you get the result you expect.

The process of getting support can take some time. The educational or medical authority in your area may want to restrict the number of diagnoses of autism in your area. But this isn't about a number – this is about need.

The old system of statements has given way to educational and health care plans which have been designed to give parents more say over how their children are helped. This puts an emphasis on schools working together with other agencies so that they are better informed about the needs of each individual child and can plan together with others at moments of transition. These can follow an autistic person or a person with other special needs to the age of twenty-five years.

Too many children are still being failed by a system that is not picking up their needs early enough. They are wrongly being labelled as disruptive or educationally weak when what they need is support and encouragement. There are many potential problems for the autistic child at school to face.

The National Autistic Society's website says that many children on the autism spectrum feel that the worst thing about being at school is being picked on or bullied. Yet so frequently this goes unnoticed, as the child is unable to describe what they have experienced or is wary of confiding in an adult who might not see it as important. This will cause a huge rise in the levels of anxiety and further strains on mental health. The majority of autistic children are not in the kind of school their parents believe best supports them. How can we as a community or parents or a church encourage the development of appropriate education?[2]

The need for safe spaces and to withdraw

Autistic people need to have a place where they can withdraw when they feel under pressure. Some schools provide rooms that are not over-stimulating, rather bland in appearance.

Some autistic people like to wear a hooded top, so that they can pull it up when they feel they want to have some kind of private space. Given the demonization of some young people with hoodies, this can be problematic on occasions, but this is important. To withdraw if even for a few minutes can make the difference between handling a situation and the autistic person going into a meltdown.

Allowing time to use this space may well help to defuse a situation. Here again, aren't there times when we all leave a room or a place, to avoid doing or saying something that we might regret? Schools should make sure that there are such places as well as a person with the responsibility for safeguarding to make sure that any autistic person is safe in that space.

Alternative provision ideas

Donkey sanctuary

Many museums and centres have become aware of their need to cater for autistic people. One model of good practice to help autistic people is the Donkey Sanctuary near Sidmouth in Devon. The staff encourage children to care for the donkeys, brushing their manes and having the sensations of touch. The sessions I observed involved an autistic person and one who does not have the condition; the team gently asked them to work together to construct a mild obstacle course subsequently to lead the donkeys around.

This enabled the autistic person to practise working with another person, to reflect on what worked and did not work (for example, they constructed a hurdle that the donkey did not jump but simply walked around!). Many have talked about the value of using the care of animals as a place to help build on social interaction and to encourage team building.

Therapy dogs

Some people have used dogs in order to bring some rest and relaxation to autistic people. As we have seen, interacting with donkeys (and horses) can have positive benefits for autistic people. The act of stroking can help to calm them and reduce their anxiety. Working with animals may be easier than working with humans, as they do not need to try to communicate directly but might do so via other senses such as looks and touch.

A difficult conversation

Some schools will challenge parents to consider if their child should continue to attend a mainstream school. The school may feel that there are needs that it cannot fulfil. Staff might be worried about the way in which other students relate to the autistic person. As parents, we need to think carefully where the best place is for our children. Some will best thrive in a special school, many will find the environment of a mainstream education constructive and challenging.

Simon and Carol had taken the decision to put Tom into a mainstream school. During reception and Year 1, no one seemed to worry about him, even though he was not hitting the targets that he should have done at around the expected times. Carol and Simon were taken by surprise by something that happened at the Year 2 parents' evening.

'Mrs Ferris would like to talk to you.'

Mrs Ferris was the head teacher. She came and sat down. 'Thanks. We want you to do some careful thinking about Tom's future.'

'Future?' Simon asked.

'We think you should consider for the good of Tom and you if this is the appropriate place for him to be.'

Simon felt a shiver go down his back. His wife looked tearful.

Mrs Ferris seemed to want to back off a little, 'We will give him all the support he needs. We just want to be sure that you are convinced that this is the right place.'

Simon and Carol had never had a doubt about this – why was it a problem for the school? Were they being helpful or were they worrying that he might cost them something in their standard assessment tests (SATs)?

Many parents have had a similar conversation. It feels as though this is one that you can never win on. If you keep your child in a primary school, they might be kept back socially and intellectually. If you send them to a special school, they might develop a more negative view about themselves, which would limit their possible achievements. Teachers – especially those who work closest with our children – should be able to ask us difficult questions like this. We may not always want them, but we need to face them. We need to find the appropriate place for each child.

However, we do not wish slavishly to accept what professionals think about our children. As parents, we know our child better than anyone else does, but there are going to be times when our faith in them might seem irrational to others. We need to be honest with ourselves and not project on to our children unrealistic expectations of who they are. We need to love them, for who they are, not who we would like them to be. We need to encourage learning but not give them unnecessary guilt if being autistic makes learning really difficult.

What matters most is appropriate education. For some, that is going to be found in specialist provision. For many, it will be within existing primary school structures, with support either one-to-one or in groups. Parents will need to pray and think hard about any changes. It is possible to go between the two sectors and that might be helpful for some. Children need a consistent set of expectations or people to help them make the best progress possible.

Christians need to be possibility thinkers. There may be barriers that cannot be fully conquered, but we don't necessarily know what these will be. We need to think more about what our children can do or might be able to do rather than to obsess over what they cannot achieve. We need to remember that the image of God is in all of us and that God can use those that others disregard. All are special in the kingdom, because all can and will serve if they live in obedience to the will of God.

The problem with 'spectrum thinking' in schools

The emphasis on spectrum thinking – on saying that everyone can show signs of being on the autistic spectrum – can be a good thing but we need to be careful. It could actually weaken the care given to those with extreme needs.

The person who says that their behaviour is 'autistic' is most likely using it as an excuse for frankly being rude. We should not allow our culture to debase the word to justify unacceptable behaviour as that will not help and support the autistic community. We will need to challenge that if it happens. If a child misbehaves, we need not immediately blame autism – there can be other reasons. Many autistic children will not display obvious behavioural features.

The spectrum idea is important to understanding the concept of autism, which encompasses a variety of learning abilities and personality traits.

Weaker students on the spectrum may have problems with maths and English, as they might find it difficult to retain language, or to understand the principle behind a number representing a concept. Abstract ideas are often quite difficult to explain, as the autistic person can have a more concrete method of thinking.

Alternatively, you might find those whose memory and understanding of the ideas is excellent. They may be able to recall vast amounts of information. They might ask unexpected questions.

Remember that the spectrum or constellation is a rough description. It is not a scale. It is designed to be open-ended, in contrast to a one-size-fits-all description. Theoretically, a child might be seen as weak but actually because of a combination of other factors could overachieve.

Meltdown at school

Transitions are bound to increase the anxiety that autistic people feel. As already mentioned, one such challenge is moving to a new school.

> *Simon was on his way home from visiting a parishioner when he had a phone call from Carol. Their son, Tom, had not come out of school. What should she do?*
>
> *He told her to go to reception, where they rang through to student support. Tom was there, angry and overcome as he had been unable to answer a question in a lesson. This had made him feel very vulnerable, especially as he had only just gone to secondary school. He had become tearful and overcome, angry at himself. He immediately had to take himself out of the situation as a way to stop his anxiety.*
>
> *Was this going to happen to Tom every day at secondary school? Actually, it did not have to be that – and it did not become like that.*
>
> *The school knew enough to be prepared for this, which was vital. They had a place where the boy could go and where it was possible to talk to someone who could help develop some calm. In the years to come, there would be other meltdowns but, as the staff were informed and experienced, they were managed well. Although distressing at the time, Tom's meltdowns did not destroy the joy he felt at school most of the time.*

Social stories

Social stories can come in the form of a series of pictures or text or combination thereof which can be used with an autistic person to help them prepare for or evaluate a situation. They can be used, for example, when dealing with a difficult situation such as bullying or bereavement.

Using a story can help give a bit of distance, which enables the person to reflect on what has happened to them. There is a lot of biblical precedence for this: consider how Nathan tells David the parable of the stolen sheep in order to make him understand the chaos of his affair with Bathsheba, or the power of the parables that Jesus uses, for example that of the Good Samaritan.

Stories can help to strengthen and develop social imagination and contribute to progress towards understanding.

Appropriate curriculum within a school

There may need to be modifications to the curriculum of individual autistic children in order to enable them to achieve all that they can. A child who is interested in the ancient world might enjoy studying Latin, getting great satisfaction from learning the verb forms. The language's logical structure will appeal to a person who looks for pattern and order.

Schools need to think about offering autistic students times to withdraw. Even if all they do is give time to mentor and support the young person, it will be worth it. Teaching in smaller groups can help. As already mentioned, sometimes current educational thinking about the need for students to learn in small groups can mean that classrooms can get very noisy, which can be quite difficult for autistic students to deal with. We need to be aware of this and make sure that schools have appropriate strategies to help them deal with it or escape for periods of quiet.

It is important to play to people's strengths. Links to industry or farms that offer work placements could help build confidence or develop skills.

Exclusions and autism

How difficult are schools for autistic children? One measure of this is how far schools are able to deal with the challenging behaviour that may arise when their needs are not being met.

According to the National Autistic Society, there is a crisis about exclusions, with autistic children being excluded frequently.[3] How far is this about the children, and how far is this about the school not being prepared and having strategies to help the children in the surroundings of school? Despite some training and many excellent SEN departments, not all schools are prepared for dealing with an autistic child. In August 2018, a UK judge ruled over a case where an autistic child had been excluded from school for one and a half days following an incident where he hit a teaching assistant with a ruler, then punched her and ended up pulling her hair. The judge ruled that the school had been wrong to exclude as 'aggressive behaviour is not a choice for children with autism'. The school should have made reasonable adjustments to make sure that this behaviour was coped with.[4] Schools will have to respond to this ruling and seek a helpful way forward.

Excellent safeguarding makes sure that students and staff are protected. At the same time the fundamental right to an education must be maintained and autistic people must not lose out because of behaviour they may not be able to control.

When you look at exclusions from school, you will find beneath the surface many students who are autistic. It is clear that some students' behaviour is enormously difficult to manage. They will be endlessly questioning the teacher (not to get one over but to make it clear what is expected). They may have some difficult relationships with other members of the class, which can become explosive. Perhaps they talk over the teacher or another student. Or they fidget – do we allow them to use a toy or even something as simple as a rubber band to help them channel their anxiety? The advice is clear – if we can reduce a student's anxiety, we should. Doing so can also reduce the tension in a classroom.

Many schools issue students with a card to show a teacher, which may allow them to leave the classroom if they feel anxiety or anger overtaking them. They are usually able to go to a room or a designated person who can give them some support. These are important as a safeguard but they are not of themselves enough.

The church needs to be supportive of both the students who are excluded and their parents. Yet we also need to be asking hard questions about how far schools can deal with students with challenging behaviour. Schools deserve our non-judgemental support and encouragement where they are genuinely doing their best to make reasonable adjustments.

Moving to college

Some autistic people will go on to college or university. They will need assistance in dealing with the transitions that will be involved in this. Should they be in a hall of residence, or should they stay with a family to have a more settled existence? These are choices that need to be faced.

How are they going to deal with public transport to and from where they are studying? What needs to be put in place in this respect?

The relatively relaxed, unstructured nature of many college and university courses may be something that can ironically feel more difficult for an autistic person to deal with. They might need help to structure their days as a means of reducing their feelings of anxiety.

Some universities and colleges will have a mentoring scheme, which will be able to provide help for the autistic person as they adapt to their new environment. Mentors can regularly check what issues they are facing and, if necessary, act as brokers between the person and the university over any difficult problems.

There are other times in life when autistic people need advocates who can speak for them in difficult situations, to ensure their needs are catered for. We will look at these in further chapters.

Reflection

Think about the successes and the failures you had at school.

- How did you deal with the failures?
- How did teachers help or hinder you?
- What were your relationships like with your classmates?
- Imagine that you did not have the words to express your needs – what difference might that have made to your experience?

Prayer

Father, we pray for those who work in schools. Give them wisdom and guidance to help their autistic students to flourish. Let every student know they are valued and accepted, whatever difficulties they have.

Amen

5

The Workplace

There are many difficulties in helping autistic people into employment. The National Autistic Society reports that only 22 per cent of autistic people are in full-time paid work.[5] However, these statistics do not take into account the likely number of as yet unidentified autistic adults who have managed to stay employed throughout their lives. There are other issues too – to what extent do autistic people receive benefits that will help them get into work, in terms of travel assistance? How far have employers followed the lead of the government in making 'reasonable adjustments' (to use the legal phrase) to help such people?

The UK Government set itself a target of halving the disability employment gap by 2020.[6] We are clearly not there yet. We need to make the case to help autistic people. We need to encourage government and employers to try ever harder to reach that goal. We could try shaming employers or pricking their social conscience.

We need to encourage shops to have policies to employ more autistic people and to see their worth as workers. We should also celebrate those who are making efforts to recruit and retain autistic staff. However, how much more success could be had if we were to broadcast some of the advantages companies might find if they employed more autistic people?

Firstly, if you were an employer, you would have someone who has a keen eye for detail: they want to get things right and will be more thorough than many others who are not on the spectrum. Seemingly repetitive tasks can feel more satisfying to a person with autism than to others. Stocking shelves or putting things together is boring for many, but for some autistic people these are satisfying tasks.

Careers in information and communication technology or in institutions such as libraries prove fulfilling too, as they rely on skills and order, with minimum social interaction. Finding the right environment for each autistic person is important. Some may be able to cope with a library but these have begun to re-invent themselves, and are no longer the havens of silence they once were.

It has rightly been observed that most of the modern world can be grateful to autistic people. Roles in developing computing and data have been helped by the autistic community, though the commonly held belief that Silicon Valley's genius is connected to a higher-than-average autistic population in the USA has been disputed.

Changes and preparations are needed to make the workplace more acceptable to autistic people. Is there too much information on notice-boards, for example? Are they too cluttered? How can the autistic person deal with unstructured time such as tea breaks or lunch-times that are part of a working day? If there is a shared eating space such as a canteen, the employer should seek to give an opportunity to eat without the noise and bustle that can happen at lunch-time.

Are tasks an employer is expecting an autistic person to undertake clearly explained, using a step-by-step approach or providing a checklist to help them achieve the required standard? I suspect that when these changes are made, many workers will find themselves more relaxed – just as adults often love a long children's talk instead of a sermon as they feel that they might be more able to understand it!

Before a person can be employed, they need to have their confidence built up and to have acquired skills that are useful in the workplace. Can we as churches offer them tasks which give them experience of the world of work if they have not yet had that?

Could we work with local charities to help with this? When I came out of university, I did not find full-time paid work for quite a time and worked for a charity for the blind that needed volunteers to help with sending out financial appeals. It was obvious to me that many of the workers who were doing this with me were people who found getting into work difficult because of their various disabilities.

The National Autistic Society is a great source of information about how to prepare for the world of work; for example, giving suggestions about how to prepare curriculum vitae. They can also help an organisation prepare to employ autistic people by arranging a workplace visit to assess what may need to change in order for it to be appropriate as a working environment, to match the 'reasonable adjustments' in law. The incoming autistic worker should have a tour around the place of employment to acquaint themselves with it before they begin their employment.

Work matters for several reasons for all of us. It can give us a sense of fulfilment, of tasks completed and some improvement to our lives or those of others. It gives us a sense of identity. Perhaps we should not always fall back on that 'What do you do?' line when we first meet someone, but it is true that work can confer an identity.

For a Christian, work is a vocation that God gives us. So if we can help a person into work, then we are helping them to fulfil one of the purposes of God for their life. Empowerment is the ultimate goal, where the person can make progress by themselves, becoming less and less dependent on others. For the autistic person, it can give not just a sense of self-worth but also provide some independence, if it is paid work. It might create the possibility of independence in some other way, perhaps leading to a move away from home or living with others in a sheltered situation.

One great advantage for autistic people is that they find the repetitious nature of much work is not the obstacle that it is to others, but is actually fulfilling in itself. It is more stimulating to them than to many non-autistic people. Some autistic people have a desire to get things right in display or in procedure that could make life better for their fellow-workers.

Work can be difficult as it inevitably comes with a whole set of social interactions that might be problematic. Employers will need to ensure that their autistic workers are treated and talked to with appropriate respect and helpfulness by their fellow-workers, as well as being given help, support, and encouragement to speak to their boss in confidence.

A workplace mentor will be a great help, a person who probably isn't their line manager but can show the autistic worker how to approach their tasks. The mentor can talk them through routines and prepare them when there are to be changes in practice. The hope is that this would avoid some problems they would otherwise face. The mentor could also help them to understand the social cues in that workplace. There is a lovely moment in an episode of *Dr Who* (while played by Peter Capaldi) when the Doctor is shown a list of things that he should not say or do to upset people needlessly.

Workers need to be prepared to be fully welcoming and accepting of autistic people, who might behave in unexpected ways. For example, as many autistic people are more perfectionist than the norm, they often need more time to complete tasks. It is important that fellow-workers do not perceive this as them being deliberately slow or awkward.

Autistic people can require both formal and informal meetings to assess where they might need assistance. Issues that seem trivial to others – such as a computer glitch or if the photocopier does not work in the normal way – might produce a great sense of anxiety to an autistic person. They will need to know in advance who they should go to for help and if there are alternatives to the way things are done. Anticipation and preparation are important to help reduce the anxiety they constantly face.

Some autistic employees need visual cues such as photographs to help them prepare. They might need to do a 'dry run' of using public transport so that they do not get anxious about this, getting used to travel. Flexible working hours may need to be agreed, so that the autistic person avoids particularly heavy commuting periods.

It is also very important that autistic people are protected from unreasonable demands and bullying behaviour. The Autism Act of 2009 protects them in the workplace and we need to make sure that the law is upheld. The Autism Strategy of 2020 seeks to develop ways in which the Act is put into practice, looking at the issues of reporting of needs, developing workforce policies, the care of autistic people by the NHS and other providers as well as helping those with ASD to participate in their local community. The 2014 Care Act and the 2014 Child and Families Act both have provisions helping people with autism. Organisations like the Citizens' Advice Bureau can be called upon for their expertise to help if there are issues. Autistic people are also covered by the equality and disability discrimination legislation that covers us all.

Everyone needs to find the right balance between work and leisure. Autistic people may find their perfectionism makes it difficult to 'turn off' from work if they do not feel they have achieved their best. They need to be encouraged to rest and see that some tasks will take experience and time to get right.

Reflection

Think of one of the places you work in or have worked at.

- How difficult would it be for an autistic person to work there?
- What changes would be needed?
- How easily could they be made?

Prayer

Father, we pray for those autistic people who are in jobs. Help their employers to be respectful of their difficulties and to encourage them. May there be justice in the workplace for all.

Amen

6

Society in General

Making public places autistic-friendly

We have seen the growth in recent years of cinemas having autism-friendly performances, where the lighting may be more consistent, the sound more moderate and where behaviour that would be less acceptable in a normal screening is allowed for. To use the government phrase, 'reasonable adjustments' can and should be made to render public places more inclusive.

The broadcaster Chris Packham backed the campaign for an autism hour in supermarkets, banks and other public spaces. He was quoted as saying, 'I rarely go into supermarkets. I find that environment challenging. That's why I am keen to back Autism Hour, those shops which offer an hour where they make the whole atmosphere a lot more relaxing for autistic people.'[7]

Many people who have autism try to avoid or limit shopping as they find the bright lights and noise too much, possibly coupled with memories of meltdowns or difficult emotions when they were last there.

Shops as diverse as Asda, Morrisons and The Entertainer toy shops have started offering shopping times that reflect the needs of autistic people. Think for a moment about the space that a supermarket can be – loud music, jostling people, a bewildering choice and the differing temperatures and smells across the shop. By lowering the lights and removing the background music, these shops have begun to think about their customers and their needs and they are to be congratulated. Many non-autistic shoppers have commented favourably on this development, feeling that it benefits them too. Very few reasonable adjustments are detrimental to the needs of the wider community!

Support from social services

Many adults with autism feel that they are not getting the support from social services that would help them to have a good life. This does give rise to political questions: with cuts to social services, are the most vulnerable under siege? While the church might be able to give support, there are structural changes that we need to highlight to make sure that those who have autism get the support they need.

At least one in three autistic adults is experiencing severe mental health difficulties due to a lack of support. We know that it is becoming fashionable for political parties to realise the crisis about mental health but now we need to hold them to account.

Social media and people with ASD

Social media is a powerful thing. For autistic people, Facebook and other forums can be a useful means of contact with others, especially if meeting people face-to-face is difficult. Connection through written words rather than having to concern themselves with social cues lessens anxiety. It can open up the possibility of connecting with others who share and understand autism. It could provide opportunities for developing friendships and other relationships. The use of services like Skype and FaceTime help autistic people to deal with communicating with people on their own terms and on a more level playing field.

However, social media can be quite destructive. A word or phrase used on social media may greatly upset others. There might be systematic bullying of a person. So we will need to make sure that autistic people are aware of the downsides as well as the possibilities.

Blogs by autistic people can be enormously empowering for them and those who seek to understand, but again there is a danger that they could make themselves vulnerable to the abuse of others if their blogging is not handled correctly. At their best, though, a blog may become the voice that is often denied, helping them to raise understanding and empathy towards autistic people.

We need to make autistic people aware of the debates around 'fake news' – that not everything that is posted is necessarily true. As many autistic people take things at face value, we need to encourage them to think about what is being presented, and why.

They need to be encouraged to be aware of the possibility of being radicalised. Recently a police officer told me that when police look at radicalisation online, they are not just concerned about faith groups or other communities, but also how autistic people could easily be manipulated. We know that a few terrorist incidents have involved people who have shown autistic traits. The extremist might offer a sense of belonging and acceptance to a person who feels excluded and powerless.

Social media is a challenge to the church and to society. We need to be models of inclusivity, of affirming that as everyone is made in the image of God, they all have dignity. If we don't offer a positive message, there will be people who very definitely will try to fill that void and if they can see a way to manipulate someone they see as weak or open to persuasion, they will do so.

Churches could offer training in the use of social media to support and encourage autistic people to use them in ways that are beneficial and not destructive to them.

There is evidence that some computer programmes such as Minecraft have encouraged people to be more creative and to develop relationships with others. For an autistic person, these could foster an expertise that others do not have.

Autistic people do need to have some online services carefully explained. While online shopping and banking services could help them by minimising their need to go into a public place where they might feel anxiety, inappropriate use of such services will cause problems.

Autism and the law

In the UK, there are a number of laws relating to the rights of autistic people about which we need to be aware. The Autism Act of 2009 was specifically targeted at autistic people. It sought to improve their access to social services and the NHS, making sure that all who asked had a right to diagnosis. The Care Act and the Child and Families Act, both of 2014, help protect rights over mental health, appropriate care by health/care professionals, employment and the criminal justice system. The 2020 Autism Strategy denotes that the government is trying to bring together various Acts, together with statutory guidance to make sure that autistic people have their rights and opportunities protected.

There are other laws that can help autistic people, such as the Human Rights Act from 1998, and the Equality Act of 2010 combined with a whole variety of laws to make sure that nothing is discriminatory. The Equality Act introduced the concept of 'reasonable adjustments', where people who were responsible for providing some service should bear in mind the needs of those who are autistic. These can extend to other public places as well.

The 'quieter hours' we mentioned with shops are an example of this, as is the special cinema performance. There should be others, such as allowing autistic people to eat in a canteen earlier or later than their work mates to avoid the noise of lunch time. Employers might also allow an autistic person to work at a different speed to others; especially if they are more anxious about checking and re-checking a particular set of tasks.

Schools allow students to leave lessons early, especially at the end of the day to enable them not to feel sensory overload at the lesson change-over time.

The Care Act of 2014 made sure that they have protection even in such actions such as buying financial arrangements. Do we have the expertise in our churches to help protect autistic people? Or do we know a good lawyer to help them?

Churches should encourage autistic people and their families to know their legal rights and to make sure that they can defend them if necessary. We should try to influence law-makers to value the rights of others and show respect for the needs of autistic people. Churches have rightly lobbied for themselves, for the developing nations – now we must also make sure that the vulnerable in our own society are cared for.

Hate crimes and autistic people

Hate crimes are directed against a particular group or person on the basis of a perceived difference relating to disability, race, religion, sexual orientation or gender identity. In 2020 there were 105,096 reported cases of hate crime, of which 8,469 were aimed at disabled people, a rise of 8 per cent on 2019.[8] Autistic people and those with learning disabilities are four times more likely than other disabled people to be the victims of hate crime, and 73 per cent of people with learning disabilities and/or autism have reported that they have been the victims of hate crime.[9] We need to make sure that this vulnerability is reduced.

Hate crimes can occur in the following areas.

1. *Verbal/written abuse.* This can include attacks on their disability or using other terms of abuse like 'paedophile'. On social media, insults include being described as odd or difficult. Entrapment via blackmail may be attempted. Autistic people may not always realise that they are being attacked and it is important to help them find appropriate ways to deal with this, where necessary involving the police and other authorities.

2. *Physical abuse.* Autistic people can be used as punch-bags by those who are unable to express their anger in other ways. Misunderstanding the attack, some autistic people may think they in some way deserve it. We need to make them aware that physical abuse is not acceptable, and to prosecute those who do this.

3. *Property.* Autistic people can be very trusting, and that can make them more vulnerable to being victims of crime. Their property may be damaged to humiliate them, but it must be respected as much as anyone else's and we need to make sure that they understand this.

4. *Intimidation/coercion.* The use of bullying and threats against an autistic person may be used as a way to gain power or to humiliate. This may be accompanied by the threat of violence or violence itself. The autistic person needs to have the support of a trusted friend/carer/parent in seeing that not all people behave fairly to others, and that they can be targeted.

5. *Sexual abuse.* An autistic person could be sexually abused because they are unable to say no or understand what might be happening to them. They may not know the law on consent or be aware of appropriate boundaries between people. We need to make sure that safeguarding provisions are put in place to help the most vulnerable. We also need to educate them about sex and relationships.

6. *Mate crime.* This is where a person pretends to be a friend to someone on the autistic spectrum in order to gain some advantage or power from the relationship. The person committing mate crime grooms the autistic person for months or years to commit a crime against them or to encourage them into a criminal act.

It is very important that autistic people have appropriate support when a crime against them is reported. They may need an appropriate adult to be with them. Police procedure can be very intimidating so it is important that every provision is made to encourage the person to feel they are valued and being cared for at a difficult time.

Crime and the autistic person

There have been historic miscarriages of justice where an autistic person has been wrongly convicted of a crime. They may have become confused while being questioned by the police, which can lead to an inappropriate or wrong sentence.

Autism cannot be an excuse for breaking the law but it is important that judges and the due process of justice take account of the condition and acknowledge that it might be a contributory factor when passing judgement. When sentencing, judges should be thoughtful about the problems that autistic people will face if they have a custodial sentence. The conditions of a prison or a detention centre may be very difficult for autistic people. Some have attempted or succeeded in committing suicide when sent to prison.

Reflection

Think about a time when you have felt vulnerable and needed support.

- How did other people help you?
- What did other people do that wasn't very helpful?
- Did faith help you deal with the situation?

Prayer

Father, we thank you for those who help to shape our society by the making of laws. May they act justly and love mercy, enabling autistic people to live safe and fulfilling lives, without the fear of discrimination or being treated with a lack of respect.

Amen

7

Helping a Family with an Autistic Person

A few years ago, the Children's Society had a great poster which featured a child with the slogan, 'What I need is a good listening to!' This seems to me to be where helping families with an autistic person needs to begin.

They need to be able to be listened to, for others to hear their frustrations and their joys, the problems and the feelings they go through. It is a feeling of being alone that most affects the parents and the autistic person. Knowing that they are being listened to is vital. Don't offer advice – give a listening ear. Try not to judge when things are said in the heat of a moment of frustration or difficulty, but give support and encouragement.

It is important to be open to learn about autism from those who are living with it or alongside it. Pastoral support in churches is important and it is best in the spirit of humility, which listens carefully to what is being said.

Offer help with practical support. Can you give a family a break, even for a few hours, from a demanding situation? The gift of time – be that to go shopping, to see friends or just to have some time alone – is one of the most important gifts you can give to a family under pressure.

Could the church offer long-term help in the support of an autistic person? One-to-one pastoral support is great but what might need to change in church and groups to help the whole family?

If a family is being overwhelmed by the bureaucracy that goes with filling in forms to get financial and other support, how can you practically help? Are there experts in social services or the law who could lend their advice? The kingdom of God is about love, justice and mercy or it is of no use to anyone. We need to live lives that show that, and supporting families dealing with autism is important.

Making sure that siblings are supported is important. How could you help the family with an autistic member in that area?

It is important that families feel accepted and welcome at church. We have seen this isn't always the case. For some families, this can be the only time in the week that they can all get out of their home together, so embrace them.

Ask the family. They will be able to tell you what they most need.

Above all, make sure that they know that they are not alone and that, however difficult the situation, God can be found there in his loving purposes.

Reflection

- The church is our family – each individual family is a part of that. How can we help and support each other?
- How can we give the gift of time to families who are living with an autistic family member?

We begin in prayer. We continue in listening. We reflect and we act in the Spirit of love.

Prayer

Father, you are the Creator of families. Grant families the patience they need to show true love to each other. Help us to support and encourage families with an autistic member, to listen and respond to their needs in the power of your Spirit.

Amen

8

How Can the Church Support People with Autism?

Ask yourself for a moment – how autism-friendly is your church? What barriers are there that would hinder autistic people from coming to your services and events? Can we encourage autistic people to feel at home with worship?

Imagine a family with a son who enthusiastically takes part in worship and, because of autism, lacks a sense of restraint. When the worship leader encourages the children to come forward, the boy is there. His parents are a little bit more Anglican and restrained. There is a moment when the boy seems to be embarrassing and perhaps is attracting more attention than normal. It is very important that he is allowed to worship God as he wants to and also that the congregation focuses. How can we square this?

As a member of the congregation, you need to show affirmation to the boy while thinking about the need not to allow behaviour that could be seen as egocentric or harmful to others who are worshipping. (This is a problem bigger than autism – think of all the times when the insensitive nature of others has hampered you in worship or when you might have been a cause of it to others.)

Churches should not be surprised that some autistic people might actually try to answer the rhetorical questions that preachers ask. A minister may need to find a new way to preach, which can be difficult.

The Evangelical Alliance published an article by Alexandra Davis about how a local church could prepare for autistic people. It contained the following: 'Our churches can sometimes be loud places: take, for example, praise and worship, with the complete band and corporate prayer. People who have autism tend to experience sensory overload, so services full of sound and people can be overwhelming.' She then gives this challenge: 'Maybe your church family could take part in regular services that strip back a lot of what you would normally do and keep it simple?'[10] She has a point and I think that a good number of the congregation might like the stripped-back service themselves!

Our churches – especially evangelical ones – can be overly busy, not giving room for quiet reflection. As well as appropriate worship spaces or services, there are other things that the church can do to help.

Prayer

A friend of mine mentioned that when it came to corporate church, their church had not acknowledged the role of parents or the needs of children with disabilities in intercessions. This did change in her church, but we need to think about this. Does the staff team at your church meet regularly to pray for pastoral needs and do they give time to those who are dealing with situations like autism? The families need to feel supported and prayer is an action that demonstrates it. Does the family with the autistic person have an email address or a phone number to help them get in contact with someone when they need urgent prayer support?

Appropriate worship

Hereford Cathedral in the UK pioneered an autism quiet hour following work by its disability access officer. They have also provided maps and ear defenders for autistic visitors to use. Hereford Cathedral discovered that others who were not autistic but liked a more reflective style of worship were helped by this. There may be some pleasing and unexpected consequences of serving the needs of autistic people.

Preparing the congregation

Interviewed in *Christianity Today* in July 2018, the American sociologist Andrew Whitehead talked about the struggles of trying to take his two non-verbal autistic children to a worship service. He had encountered a differing set of reactions, many of which were negative. He cited one parent who had been asked what was the point of taking their child to worship as 'They clearly won't get anything from it'. (That could apply to most of us some Sundays!) He told too of a member of another congregation who was concerned that the parent should just get their autistic child under control, mistaking their behaviour for being naughty.

Whitehead concludes that a congregation will need to be prepared and they will need some training.[11] It is important too that ministers speak up for the rights of all to come to worship. Children with the greatest need for a supportive community were the most likely to feel unwelcome.

Pastoral support

Is there someone in your church who can provide some pastoral support to families? For example, at a practical level, could your church organise baby-sitting occasionally so that parents can have a night out? Everyone needs to have a listening ear, someone with whom you can share the difficulties that parents of an autistic child face. People in families with autistic children or adults will have a number of tensions and pressure points, and will need help.

Befriending

As well as formal pastoral support, there is just the general befriending. In our congregation, we have an autistic person who has been befriended by a number of people. Often, they have taken the person on trips in order to strengthen their relationship with them. Befriending requires time and effort, but is worth it. It will require careful planning. Any sensory issues the autistic person may have will need to be checked so that they are taken to venues where they will feel safe, and planning ahead using social stories to outline what they may expect will be helpful.

Suppers

One of the most effective supports we have enjoyed as parents is the organising of a series of suppers which have brought together families who have autistic children. This enables people to chat about their experiences. As we are at different points – with children of different ages – this means we are able to help each other with the journey. Those of us who have come to terms with a diagnosis are able to help those at the start of the journey. Those who have pre-secondary school children are able to hear the wisdom and experience of those who have gone through that stage and moved onto later stages.

This can be a hope-giving experience as the possibilities as well as the problems become visible. These social occasions can be very effective in helping people not feel isolated in the issues they are dealing with.

Care for adults

For over twenty years, there has been a group within our church where people with a variety of additional needs can meet together. Some are church members, some are not but all are shown love by the care of the group. This has been a major but barely noticed work in the church that I worship in but it is an act of love. What has been interesting about this is that it started with people then in their teenage years, but is now supporting people who are autistic and those with other conditions in their forties. This work may need to be long-term and that takes quite some commitment. It is an act of Christian service which isn't always lauded but is vital work for the kingdom.

One-to-one support

Some people do not easily fit into a group and may prefer to develop relationships with individuals. Do we notice such things, and are we willing to do something about them? This can mean a great deal to the person who is receiving the support. Many churches are so governed by the principle of encouraging people into home groups that they need to realise this does not suit everyone; individual mentoring or discipleship may be more helpful. (I think many people not on the autistic spectrum prefer this approach!)

Sharing good practice

If your church is giving support to autistic people in some way, share your methods with other churches, network meetings, deanery/diocesan synods or annual meetings, so that others can benefit from them. Put them on your church website. Churches often struggle to think of approaches but if we share what has worked in our context, it could be something that can be reproduced in another place, or the idea might give rise to another. We should not copyright a method we can find of sharing and supporting people in any context, let alone this one!

Find out about the latest ideas in support in the secular world

Use ideas from the secular world about ways to support autistic people, and to help the church be appropriate in its support. Knowing what the legal situation is for autistic people is really valuable. Key workers such as youth workers, the pastoral team or those with specialised ministries need to update their understanding of the issues. This is a vital part of safeguarding which we need to regularly prepare ourselves for.

Social enterprise

Some churches may well have the resources and people with skills to help develop a social enterprise, which can provide work and a purposeful activity for those who find the usual world of work difficult to enter. Some churches run cafes or tea shops – can an autistic person be employed there? What changes would make sure that was possible?

Training

Are the leaders of the children's and youth work prepared to meet with autistic people? Given that some autistic youngsters ask really difficult questions, they will need to be prepared! A leader must be informed so that they can model Christian, accepting love to the person. Their influence can help other young people who might feel frustrated, annoyed or even scared by autistic people to begin to see that all people are included in the love of God's kingdom.

There are courses such as the NCFE Level 2 Certificate in Understanding Autism, designed to help train and inform people in a care home, but which can be useful training for parents so that they are more aware of the help they might need and the issues their autistic offspring will face.

Supporting those without a diagnosis

After over forty years in a church, my feeling is that churches are often safe places for autistic people. However, not everyone is aware that they are so. Could it be that a more senior member of the congregation who does not like change or cannot handle a livelier service is just showing cultural or age-related views, or do they reflect something deeper?

The writer Gillian Drew was twenty-eight before she was diagnosed as autistic but there have been others who have received diagnoses much later in life. We need to help those who receive a late diagnosis to cope with the great change. They might feel confused or relieved by suddenly having a way to understand themselves. As Gillian says, she was just sent away from the centre with a leaflet, which was not sufficient for her to understand what autism meant.

I would suggest that many people without a diagnosis have been a great help to the church. They are the sort of people who have an eye for detail in the church accounts. They might be able to spot issues in the building before the rest of the congregation. They might be bell ringers (lots of mathematical patterns to love there) or an organist or musician.

They might be subject to depression, needing support. They might be less willing to bend if something needs to change. A church leader who wants to move a congregation on can find this quite difficult to deal with. Such people can, if you are a church leader, be your biggest support or your worst critic; or even more confusingly, both at the same time!

Do not try to diagnose another person; leave that to the professionals. You might need to sensitively encourage someone to find help, or to give support to their partner.

Show love and compassion to all! Be aware too that autism isn't a magic-bullet explanation for difficult people. Some people are difficult because they are difficult – not because they are autistic!

Reflection

- How many ideas mentioned in this chapter could your church begin to put into practice? Even one idea is worth trying as it will make you a more loving community.
- How welcoming is your worship to people with autism?
- How could your church help autistic people who might not come to church, and their families?

Prayer

Father, we pray that your church will be a place of acceptance and love for all, where autistic people can feel valued and worship you.

Amen

9

The Strengths and Joys of Autism

We have considered in this book a good many of the complications and difficulties that an autistic person and their carers might face. Yet it is important to remember that there is another part of the story, a set of positives that might emerge.

These could include the following:

1. An autistic person may well have a *devotion to the truth*. We live in a world where we often tolerate more untruth or lies than we should. The autistic person will often want to challenge that. There are of course times when issues are difficult or complicated but sometimes straightness of thinking will see through what is not very helpful. This is one of the reasons why I suspect – but can never prove – that some Old Testament prophets might have been on the spectrum. It is the reason why in our age Greta Thunberg has been so effective in capturing attention to our need to do something urgently about climate change.
2. *Retentive memories.* Those who are verbal with autism often have incredible memories, able to include great detail about events. They are much less likely to misremember key moments than those who are neurotypical.

3. *A desire for order.* The need for order and routine that can be seen as negative could be a call to get organised. How many of us have chaotic houses in need of a good tidying-up, or need to do a little more thoughtful planning about our relationships?

4. *Empathy and sensitivity.* I am increasingly convinced that the suggestion that autistic people do not feel empathy is an overstatement, and that many actually have such developed empathy that it can cause them distress. Adam Smith's work,[12] among that of others, suggests that the autistic person has an overwhelming sense of empathy that is often made even more difficult for them personally by the problems they have expressing their feelings. They feel the pain of someone else much more literally than the kind of metaphorical 'I do understand' that many of us might say to – for example – someone who is bereaved.

   Going back to Greta, her campaign to highlight climate change happened as a result of a high degree of empathy. She says that as she sat in a geography lesson where she was given facts about the damage humanity had done to the environment, the facts produced in her a very deep and emotional response to the issue which her classmates did not share. I have read commentators who have suggested that this was a weakness; she made something emotional that should have been objectively dealt with. But is over-feeling something better than under-feeling it? I would love to be told I felt too much rather than too little.

5. *Focus.* Attention to detail seems to me to be a gift, a great strength. I am personally not that good at seeing the finer points of something. This is why many autistic people have been able to help with the development of mathematics and computing or have shown a great deal of ability to find

solutions to difficult problems. Many employers like autistic people who can give their full attention to what others might miss.

6. *A different way of looking at things.* Autistic people can give a very different insight into the world. They can be very individual, although special interests or obsessions may sometimes fascinate them too much. There is in our age an interest in trivia and people often delight in obscure or specialist knowledge. People who do not fit the norms or expected behavioural patterns can be seen as charming and different. We need to celebrate the differences that there are among us.

7. *Slower living.* Much of modern life is lived at a very fast pace. Autism may well call us to slow down as we accommodate the needs of others. It may involve living at a slower pace if you are a carer. This need not always be a negative but might be a positive that enables us to see the world in a new way. Autistic people can tend to live in the moment – which is a good thing, rather than being obsessed with the future as many neurotypical people are.

8. *Freedom from cynicism.* Many autistic people have a lack of cynicism about the world that their neurotypical counterparts do not have. They are willing to trust people and see people's motives as good. This can be a weakness – but there is much to be said for not living in constant suspicion of other people's motives or endlessly questioning the way they speak, seeing possible hidden meanings. At one level, that seems to be quite appealing!

It is right that this book should draw attention to the difficulties but it is appropriate to highlight the positives about autism. Being friends with an autistic person or part of a family with one or more autistic people can be fulfilling, can be fun and can make those who are not autistic less selfish and more aware of the needs of others.

Relationships like marriage and having a family do show us the selfish side of our nature but are also places where we truly learn to love, to give and not to count the cost. While we must not idealise this, we equally need to avoid the temptation to make it all about doom and gloom. Autism is a condition that can teach us to live better and to learn from those that society might often forget or try to ignore.

10

Autism – Towards a Theology

Where do we go to develop a theology of autism? These are some thoughts which build upon the Bible's teachings. When we want to form such a theology, we need to listen to the ideas and the insights for whom it is most necessary – autistic people and those who support them.

Luther once argued that the best way for workers to develop a theology relevant to their concerns was to talk about the Bible with others who were at the same stage as they were. So I speak as a father of an autistic child – my context. The theology I develop relates to this context, as well as my understanding.

All theologies are informed by our understanding of the Christian tradition here and now, but they are also governed by the world-views of the days we live in as well as our own experience. We may get part way to the truth. We are looking in the mirror that Paul talks about in 1 Corinthians 13 – we only see in part. However, we need to begin somewhere so here are some directions, some pointers along the way. The Bible and other parts of Christian tradition can help us to construct an approach. All practice needs to be informed by theology and all theology needs to be earthed in experience as well as reflection.

Where do we look to help us with this?

1 Kenosis

The word *kenosis* means 'emptying'; especially in biblical thought, the self-emptying of God to be in Jesus. As we read in Philippians 2:6–8:

> Who, being in very nature God,
>   did not consider equality with God something to be used to
>   his own advantage;
> rather, he made himself nothing
>   by taking the very nature of a servant,
>   being made in human likeness.
> And being found in appearance as a man,
>   he humbled himself
>   by becoming obedient to death –
>   even death on a cross!

The Son of God empties himself to become the human Jesus. God limits himself to the human form. God disables himself when he takes human form – no 'omni' word will now work. You know the omni words – omnipresent (God is everywhere), omniscient (he is all-knowing), omnipotent (he is all-powerful). No, this is God as the vulnerable, the one who removes power and comes to be with the people of earth in the form of a baby. This is the word made flesh. The word is spoken, but often misunderstood. The word is limited.

Jesus can understand the sensation of misunderstanding, and has taken this experience into God, which means he can identify with us when we share this experience.

The American theologian Nancy Eiesland has used the phrase, 'the disabled God'.[13] *Kenosis* is a disabling, an emptying and becoming vulnerable. This is an important and affirming metaphor the church should take more time to explore, rather than continually referring only to the mighty God.

God takes on the ability to feel, to be human. Incarnation is a sign of the humility of God, choosing to limit himself. Autism isn't a choice but it is limiting. God can understand limitations. God chose to disable himself. In doing so, he understands the frustrations of being human from the inside.

2 The suffering servant

The servant songs of Isaiah tell us of a messiah who will be misunderstood, whom people will reject and see as nothing, a suffering servant sent from God and – in Christian theology – a prophecy of Jesus. One experience of many autistic people is a sense of being rejected and not understood. The language of the servant might be helpful to reflect on: Isaiah 53:1–5.

Jesus understands that rejection, as he experienced it. Autism can be characterised by rejection, pain and alienation – which we should challenge as Christians, to make sure that we do not perpetuate such attitudes. We offer love in the name of Christ, a love rooted in acceptance.

3 The wordless Lazarus

In his book, *Dethroning Mammon*, Archbishop Justin Welby picks up on a remark of Jean Vanier that perhaps Lazarus was disabled, or had a learning difficulty.[14] For example, Lazarus does not speak anywhere in the gospels. He is not mentioned when Jesus tells Martha to learn from Mary, who sits at his feet to listen to the master.

Why does Lazarus not speak? I wonder, was he perhaps autistic?

There is a time that is even more surprising in the narratives where Lazarus does not talk. John 11 tells us that he died, and recounts the subsequent miracle of Jesus, who restores Lazarus to life. But we do not hear from Lazarus after his resurrection by Jesus. Isn't it odd that there is no reference to his response to the miracle of the new start he has received? Surely he should speak, to praise, to celebrate the miracle that has happened to him? Was he unable to speak?

The gospel accounts establish that Martha and Mary are sisters of Lazarus, sharing their home with him, which might suggest they are his carers. At that time and in that culture they would have expected to be either married or identified as widows, which the texts about them do not mention.

We can never be sure that the silent Lazarus is the autistic man of the Bible. No diagnosis is possible; autism as a condition had not been identified by the people of the time. Yet the silence is a really interesting clue to the possibility of his being an autistic man. If that is the case, one of Jesus' closest friends can become a source of inspiration for us in a new and hitherto unexpected way. Remember too that Jesus weeps for Lazarus – he could therefore be showing the compassion and the friendship we know Jesus showed to other disabled people, and which characterised his miracles.

4 The image of God

When I was studying for the NCFE Level 2 Certificate in Understanding Autism, the course paid much attention to human rights law as the way to protect the rights of the disabled and autistic. Laws and declarations are good – but there is something much more important to the Christian than any of this.

It is contained in the creation story:

So God created mankind in his own image,
  in the image of God he created them;
  male and female he created them. (Gen. 1:27)

All humans are made in the image of God – therefore it follows, all have a dignity and a purpose, whether they are autistic or not. Genesis 1:27 is a key for theology about any human experience or attempt to create a doctrine of humankind.

All people have dignity and purpose. They were created to glorify God and as the Westminster Confession says, 'enjoy him forever'. Just as this verse from Genesis clearly shows that male and female are made in the image of God, so too are all the people of the world. All can know God and in their own way have a relationship with him. There are no ifs and buts.

Whatever we look like, each one of us has talents that will help us to realise that there is more to life than appearances. The idea of the image of God inside of us shows that we are all capable of being creative and reflecting God's qualities.

For the Christian, however limited or locked in a person might seem, there is a spiritual side, a constant possibility of an encounter with God. We were made spiritual beings, something that is not true of even the smartest ape!

Jewish philosopher Martin Buber's book, *I and Thou*,[15] has been a source of inspiration for many Christians. Buber says that life is about relationships. There are the 'I' and 'You' relationships of human community – but the connection between two human beings is only one line in a three-sided triangle.

A relationship between a pair must include two other lines – which connect the 'I' and the 'You' to a 'Thou'. The 'Thou' is God. For Christians, the relationships we have must always be seen in the context of the one that interprets all others. When we are living with an autistic person, the triad of impairments is another set of three which can have a profound effect on all of the I–You and the I–Thou relationships.

In the 1960s Ronald Goldman found that many children – not only those on the autistic spectrum – were finding God-talk difficult as they were often failing to grasp metaphor.[16] We must learn a way of speaking about God which will be relevant to a person who is struggling to express themselves. We need to use some of the traditional pictures such as God as a father but to explain them in a way that is understandable and able to be transformative.

Language and belief can build community and a sense of the sacred, and we need to make sure that we are doing all we can to let this happen. Yes, we will fail and our efforts may be incomplete. But trust yourself to God and the kingdom will break through, sometimes despite you as well as because of you.

The image of God is about being found in community, not being isolated. In our interactions, we find God. In all humanity, we can find signs – what the Christian singer Bruce Cockburn calls 'rumours of glory'. And I mean – *all* of us.

5 Redemption

All people need the redemption of the cross. Jesus suffered and died for sinners and with sinners, understanding the pains and frustrations caused by the sin and suffering of the world.

Paul is quite clear that we all are in need of salvation. In 1 Timothy 1:15–16 we read:

> Here is a trustworthy saying that deserves full acceptance: Christ Jesus came into the world to save sinners – of whom I am the worst. But for that very reason I was shown mercy so that in me, the worst of sinners, Christ Jesus might display his immense patience as an example for those who would believe in him and receive eternal life.

This is a God who knows about the pain of Good Friday from the inside. When someone is suffering, we must go with them to their Good Friday and accept their pain. We need to remind each other that Easter will come, but it will not come easily. We need to show to each other the tender love that our Saviour showed.

The pain that parents might feel at the times of diagnosis, as well as the pains that an autistic person might suffer from the rejections and misunderstandings of others, are known in the heart of God. He does not sit by dispassionately: he has had his heart and his body broken.

6 Resurrection and final purpose

All people are incomplete and not what they should be. We have the Christian hope that will transform all of us in our weakness. We have the promise that he will 'wipe every tear from their eyes' (Rev. 21:4). The limitations of our bodies – like illness and death, and including disability – will be overcome, transformed in the light of the all-powerful God's renewal of creation.

The resurrection appearances of Jesus give us a clue to how our bodies and minds will be in the completeness of the kingdom. We will be like ourselves but more so. Resurrection is the promise of a new start, a new creation made visible, tangible.

In one sense, we need to see that autism isn't as far away from us as we might think. *All* human experience is limited, is incomplete. We *all* fail to communicate totally with each other. We *all* struggle with social interactions at times. We may have obsessions that harm us. The triad of impairments of autism is in all of us to some degree. We must be careful not to overstate this, but there are echoes in everyone of which we need to be aware.

We will never understand all the suffering in the world, but whatever we can do to bring the kingdom of God into the world, we must do in the power of the Spirit. You may be reading this with real frustration at the autism you or someone you love has experienced, wanting me to give a simple answer. I cannot. But I know this from my own experience: the God who wants to wipe away my tears is the God who will be with you every time you cry, embracing you and loving you. He is the God whose purpose is for our good, for our fulfilment, not for the brokenness we experience.

For many parents with autistic children with little or no communication seemingly possible, the idea of a radical transformation which will make them 'complete' is a concept that will transform the difficulty of present reality. However, there are others who might struggle with this – is the current body/mind enough?

All people within time are incomplete. We shall all be raised and we shall all be changed. God in his love will not destroy personalities but he will perfect. We will be recognisable to each other and made all that we are intended to be. There will be no lack in heaven, there will be no problem. In one sense, it is a sign of love and acceptance just as they are if we don't wish to remove autism from our children or friends. However, because of the advantages, do we really not want people to be all that they can? God's purpose is ultimately for perfection, to see us as we should be, not as we are. Yet there is a paradox here: Jesus' wounds show up on his resurrected body. Heaven might not 'cure' autism but instead the prejudice, the impatience that does not see it as another way of thinking, another way of engaging with the mystery of life.

7 The problems of communication

The problem of true communication is not confined to autistic people – it is universal. Can we ever truly communicate with each other, regardless of whether we are neurotypical or neurodiverse?

The world seems to be obsessed with communication and yet mistrusts that at a real human level we can ever really communicate with each other. This reminds me of the story of the Tower of Babel (Gen. 11:1–9). The arrogance of humanity is turned on its head as different languages develop because of people's rejection of God. The arrogance of Babylon, whose population would rather trust in their technology than the Lord God, is mocked. They bring a judgement on their own heads. It would take the story of Pentecost to reverse this.

The low view of language in the story of the Tower of Babel suggests that we are conning ourselves that we ever really say anything to anyone else. I don't share this negative approach. Of course, one individual can never truly share all the depth of meaning possible, even in the simplest of sentences such as 'I love you.' Yet it does seem to me that two lovers don't just need words anyway; sheer body language and the look in the eyes of another speaks volumes. If philosophers really believe language is useless, what is the point in ever speaking, ever writing philosophy itself? I prefer the approach to language that says real communication is not only a possibility, it is the reality, but with some limits.

In his book *Personal Knowledge*, Michael Polanyi talks about how language is the key to enabling human beings to obtain knowledge beyond that of animals.[17] We are who we are because we speak it – and when that is difficult, it is a major problem not just for us as individuals but for those around us.

For Polanyi, it is not a game: language really helps to shape reality, and it *is* reality. An autistic person may lack language, but that is not to say that they cannot know profound realities such as the love of God in their lives.

For the Christian, the Tower of Babel has been reversed by the pouring out of the Holy Spirit at Pentecost. True communication is had; the tongues of Pentecost are not ecstatic hidden languages that a Gnostic might take pride in. They are the reverse of Babel; the power is given to humans to really know each other. This is, to me, central to the Christian hope. There are limitations on language which the autistic person might experience but we all at times do so as well.

The autistic person might have only a few sounds to communicate with, but they can be used with profound effect. True communication is rooted in the Holy Spirit, who is the reconciler and the one who brings the new creation into the hearts, minds and tongues of all people who seek him.

Some people have pointed to the story of Nicodemus in John 3 as perhaps revealing that the great religious leader of the Jews showed signs of a lack of understanding of metaphor. When Jesus tells him that he will have to be born again to appreciate spiritual truth, Nicodemus is very confused. Can he not 'get it' because he is autistic? This could possibly be one reason for his confusion.

8 The Christian virtue of love

When Jesus is asked which commandment is the greatest, he says to love God and your neighbour. The neighbour could be a Good Samaritan, he says in his parable. The people that others had rejected turned out to be the true vehicle of the purposes of God. The qualities of love will be necessary for dealing with all humans, and therefore apply to the care of autistic people. Remember what Paul writes in 1 Corinthians 13:4–8:

> Love is patient, love is kind. It does not envy, it does not boast, it is not proud. It does not dishonour others, it is not self-seeking, it is not easily angered, it keeps no record of wrongs. Love does not delight in evil but rejoices with the truth. It always protects, always trusts, always hopes, always perseveres. Love never fails.

Remember that the word used for love here is *agape*, the selfless, giving love that characterises God, especially shown in the sacrifice on the cross. Paul teaches us that we have a responsibility to help others in Galatians 6:2: 'Carry each other's burdens, and in this way you will fulfil the law of Christ.'

We may find that we need to encourage autistic people to work on forgiving love, as the obsessional part of their nature might make a wrong seem unforgivable. We will need to model this to them and show them love when they are not being reasonable. That is the classic calling of Christian love – 'love to the loveless shown' as the hymn writer puts it.

As we encounter Scripture and our situations, there are many other texts that we could consider to develop a theology of autism. It can, however, be summarised as: God creates everyone and gives everyone dignity. We need to act and live on this principle. Use of neutral titles like 'neurodiverse' and 'neurotypical' might help to reduce the worst of prejudices but the transformative love of God is even more powerful. Love shows the dignity of the human person better than a thousand statements.

9 The prophetic tradition

We will need to be people who challenge for autistic people, and that will involve at times being critics of society and the church where it is failing them. It is not difficult to see in some of the Old Testament prophets possible autism or Asperger's syndrome. Think of some of the actions they do in order to attract attention. Think of the intense personalities they have. However, we should not diagnose people from thousands of years ago. Of course autistic people existed in biblical times, but we cannot be sure how far they are reflected in the biblical traditions. We are at best making guesses (like the one about Lazarus) or drawing analogies between then and now.

The prophetic tradition and the concept of the kingdom of God in the teaching of Jesus call us to two considerations:

1. The injustice and godlessness of the moment. How the society we live in fails to match God's love. How obedience to his word and the care of the vulnerable are railed against, although what God requires is clearly explained.

2. The hope for a better future. This isn't a vague hope – it is a definite, to-come moment. When we consider what heaven and earth will be when we live in accordance with the will of God then we will see the transformation we need to. Unless we are both critical of the present and inspired by the hope, we shall not truly be people of the promise.

Being kingdom people, we will not accept it when our brothers and sisters are treated as less than human or labelled in a way to make them powerless. No – we will challenge the structures that do not allow all to flourish and we will do all we can to support social righteousness to make sure that all are truly cared for.

A theology based on liberation

We know that Scripture has sometimes been used by the powerful to reinforce their power – be that by white slave-owners, the rich, or men, for example. A theology of autism has to be about liberation. What is this liberation? It is to remove stigma from autism, to not see it as enslaving. It is to remove pity and replace this with compassion. It is to see those areas in church and life in society where autistic people do not enjoy true freedom and help them to pursue that. It is to learn to listen to autistic people. The best person of all to develop a theology of autism is not a neurotypical, middle-aged, university-educated man – it is someone who daily wakes, conscious that they experience the world in a different way from other people, often feeling anxious in a way I can never fully understand but try to empathise with.

Like all theologies of liberation, we will need to begin by explaining what the slavery of autism could mean and calling upon all to reflect on how they might be adding to that by their actions or words.

Like all theologies of liberation, it should reflect on Isaiah 61:1:

> The Spirit of the Sovereign Lord is on me,
>> because the Lord has anointed me
>> to proclaim good news to the poor.
> He has sent me to bind up the broken-hearted,
>> to proclaim freedom for the captives,
>> and release from darkness for the prisoners.

They should bear in mind the words of Micah 6:8:

> He has shown you, O mortal, what is good.
>> And what does the Lord require of you?
> To act justly and to love mercy
>> and to walk humbly with your God.

How Jesus treated people who needed healing

Jesus always treated people with disabilities with respect: he treated them as human beings. The precise needs of a person were asked: 'What do you want?' They are not nameless pieces of data or quotas; they are people to bring to Jesus and to be helped. We should not expect to receive a cure for autism, but the love of God who treats all with dignity is seen in Jesus.

We can do nothing less. We need to live the kingdom of God's values, where everyone is valuable.

I hope that these theological reflections will help as you care for, minister to or support autistic people.

Prayer

Father, help us to use knowledge of the Scriptures and your grace to us to develop an understanding of the theological issues that autism raises. Help us to be people of the promise, sharing your love and justice with all.

Amen

Afterword

Reading this book has been a time to stop and reflect on what has happened to you if you are the parent of an autistic child or to think about how we can make our churches friendlier for autistic individuals.

You will live out the theology too: live it out to help everyone. When we become more willing to learn from and be supportive of autistic people, we will also bring about the changes that will offer everyone a little bit more of the kingdom of God in action.

Glossary of Key Terms

Advocacy – speaking up for an autistic person to make sure that their legal and human rights are protected

Anxiety – the condition of being anxious, worried or fearful which is often heightened in autistic people

Asperger's syndrome – the syndrome defined from the work of Hans Asperger by Lorna Wing, as the characteristics of high levels of intelligence in people who have autism

Attention deficit hyperactivity disorder – a condition in which a person cannot control their attention, features of which closely overlap with the autism spectrum

Autism – the term given to describe the condition of people who seem to be characterised by the triad of impairment; comes from the Greek *autos* (meaning 'self')

Autism spectrum constellation / continuum / disorder – a way of seeing autism as a condition that has a variety of different aspects, which affect people to different degrees and in different ways

Dyspraxia – difficulty in using tools and in general co-ordination

Dyslexia – a processing disorder which makes the process of reading difficult

Echolalia – literally 'repeating tongue', the repetitive copying of sounds or words

Education, health and care plan – a plan designed to help and support individuals with additional needs from birth to the age of twenty-five with many agencies – schools, hospitals and youth services, for example

Empathy – the ability to understand the emotional states of others, which may be different for people with autism

Epilepsy – a brain condition where normal functions of the brain can be interrupted by seizures

High-functioning autism – an outdated term for autistic people who have conditions like Asperger's syndrome where there are not necessarily any educational issues

Hypersensitivity – the condition in which a person might be more than normally subject to feeling pain or exceptionally sensitive to light or noise

Hyposensitivity – the condition in which people may feel less sensitivity than expected, and are therefore less likely to react to loud noises, strong tastes like garlic, etc. These people may engage in sensory seeking behaviour such as touching, tasting or poking objects/people.

Makaton – a system of communication using signs and symbols, to encourage communication with those who find verbal communication difficult

Neurodiverse – people with conditions that may reflect the autistic spectrum or less common neurological conditions; the term 'diverse' is seen as encouraging a more positive attitude to these differences, rather than seeing them as disabling

Neurotypical – people who are not on the autistic spectrum

Obsession – an interest that can often exclude all others

Obsessive compulsive disorder – the condition in which a person repeats an action such as washing (for fear of germs) or checking locks

Pica – the chewing or eating of substances that are not normally eaten, often as a way of dealing with anxiety but sometimes as a sensory seeking behaviour

Proprioception – a person's awareness of their own body, a weakened sense of which seems to be prevalent in autistic people and may again present as sensory seeking behaviour

Sensory overload – a sensation of the senses being strained by too many emotions or sensations, possibly leading to anxiety

Sensory processing disorder – the feeling of being overcome when trying to deal with information coming through touch, taste, smell, hearing and seeing

Stimming – compulsive and repeated behaviour of a physical nature, such as the flapping of hands, making noises or rocking movements, as a way to reduce feelings of anxiety or stress or meet sensory needs

Triad of impairment – the combination of differences in three skills – communication, social interaction and imagination

Notes

Part One

1   Leo Kanner, 'Autistic Disturbances of Affective Contact', *Nervous Child* 2 (1943): pp. 217–50.
2   Richard Pollack, *The Creation of Dr B: A Biography of Bruno Bettelheim* (New York: Simon & Schuster, 1996).
3   Giulia Rhodes, 'Autism: A mother's labour of love', The Guardian (24 May 2011) https://www.theguardian.com/lifeandstyle/2011/may/24/autistic-spectrum-disorder-lorna-wing (accessed 29 July 2021).
4   Simon Baron-Cohen, *Mindblindness: An Essay on Autism and Theory of Mind* (London: MIT Press, 1997).
5   Maureen S. Durkin et al., 'Autism Spectrum Disorder among US Children (2002–2010): Socioeconomic, Racial, and Ethnic Disparities', *American Journal of Public Health* (Nov. 2017), published online Oct. 2017.
6   You can read more about the UK Government's thinking about the care of autistic people at: https://www.gov.uk/government/publications/think-autism-an-update-to-the-government-adult-autism-strategy (accessed 31 Aug. 2021).
7   Lorna Wing and Judith Gould, 'Severe Impediments of Social Interaction and Associated Abnormalities in Children: Epidemiology and Classification', *Journal of Autism and Developmental Disorders* 9 (1979): pp. 11–29.

8   Hannah Devlin, 'Thousands of Autistic Girls and Women "Going Undiagnosed" due to Gender Bias', *The Guardian* (14 Sept. 2018) https://www.theguardian.com/society/2018/sep/14/thousands-of-autistic-girls-and-women-going-undiagnosed-due-to-gender-bias (accessed 31 Aug. 2021).

9   Quoted in Devlin, 'Thousands of Autistic Girls'.

10 Carrie Arnold, 'The Invisible Link between Autism and Anorexia', *Spectrum News* (17 Feb. 2016) https://www.spectrumnews.org/features/deep-dive/the-invisible-link-between-autism-and-anorexia/ (accessed 29 Jul. 2021).

11 Elisabeth Kübler-Ross, *On Death and Dying: What the Dying Have to Teach Doctors, Nurses, Clergy and Their Own Families* (London: Routledge, 2008).

Part Two

1   Tara Leniston and Rhian Grounds, *Coming Home to Autism: A Room-by-Room Approach to Supporting Your Child at Home after ASD Diagnosis* (London: Jessica Kingsley, 2018).

2   For more information see *Dealing with bullying – a guide for parents and carers* by the National Autistic Society, https://www.autism.org.uk/advice-and-guidance/topics/bullying/bullying/parents (accessed 15 Sept. 2021).

3   Sarah-Jane Critchley, 'Autistic pupils and exclusions', *National Autistic Society* (21 Jan. 2019) https://www.autism.org.uk/advice-and-guidance/professional-practice/autism-exclusion (accessed 15 Sept 2021).

4   Katherine Sellgren, 'School Exclusion of Autistic Boy Unlawful, Judge Rules', *BBC News education report* (14 Aug. 2018) https://www.bbc.co.uk/news/education-45182213 (accessed 23 Jul. 2021).

5   National Autistic Society, 'New shocking data highlights the autism employment gap' (19 Feb. 2021) https://www.autism.org.uk/what-we-do/news/new-data-on-the-autism-employment-gap (accessed 16 Sept. 2021).

6   Disability at Work, 'A tale of two commitments' (2017) https://www.disabilityatwork.co.uk/research-areas/disability-measurement-and-target/a-tale-of-two-commitments/ (accessed 16 Sept. 2021).

7   Quoted in 'The National Autistic Society's Autism Hour Held in Shops in Salisbury', *Salisbury Journal* (11 September 2018), https://www.salisburyjournal.co.uk/news/16831826.national-autistic-societys-autism-hour-held-shops-salisbury/ (accessed 31 Aug. 2021).

8   Home Office statistics report, 'Hate Crime, England and Wales, 2019 to 2020' (13 Oct. 2020) https://www.gov.uk/government/statistics/hate-crime-england-and-wales-2019-to-2020 (accessed 28 Oct. 2020).

9   Dimensions (UK) Ltd, 'How often are disability hate crimes committed?' (2021) https://dimensions-uk.org/get-involved/campaigns/say-no-autism-learning-disability-hate-crime-imwithsam/know-more/often-disability-hate-crimes-committed/ (accessed 27 Jul. 2021).

10 Alexandra Davis, 'Making Church More Accessible', *Evangelical Alliance* (1 Jul. 2018) https://www.eauk.org/news-and-views/making-church-more-accessible (accessed 23 Jul. 2021).

11 David Briggs, 'US Churches Exclude Children with Autism, ADD/ADHD', *Christianity Today* (20 Jul. 2018) https://www.christianitytoday.com/ct/2018/july-web-only/study-us-churches-exclude-children-with-autism-addadhd.html (accessed 31 Aug. 2021).

12 Adam Smith, 'Emotional Empathy in Autism Spectrum Conditions: Weak, Intact, or Heightened?' *Journal of Autism and Developmental Disorders*, 39 (2009): pp. 1747–8.

13 Nancy L. Eiesland, *The Disabled God: Toward a Liberatory Theology of Disability* (Nashville: Abingdon Press, 1995).

14 Justin Welby, *Dethroning Mammon: Making Money Serve Grace* (London: Bloomsbury, 2016).

15 Martin Buber, *I and Thou* (New York: Simon & Schuster, 2008).

16 Ronald Goldman, *Readiness for Religion* (London: Routledge, 1969).

17 Michael Polanyi, *Personal Knowledge: Towards a Post-Critical Philosophy* (Abingdon: Routledge, 1998).

Bibliography

Arnold, Carrie. 'The Invisible Link between Autism and Anorexia', *Spectrum News* (17 Feb. 2016) https://www.spectrumnews.org/features/deep-dive/the-invisible-link-between-autism-and-anorexia/ (accessed 29 Jul. 2021).

Baron-Cohen, Simon. *Mindblindness: An Essay on Autism and Theory of Mind* (London: MIT Press, 1997).

Briggs, David. 'US Churches Exclude Children with Autism, ADD/ADHD', *Christianity Today* (20 Jul. 2018) https://www.christianitytoday.com/ct/2018/july-web-only/study-us-churches-exclude-children-with-autism-addadhd.html (accessed 31 Aug. 2021).

Buber, Martin. *I and Thou* (New York: Simon & Schuster, 2008).

Critchley, Sarah-Jane. 'Autistic pupils and exclusions', *National Autistic Society* (21 Jan. 2019) https://www.autism.org.uk/advice-and-guidance/professional-practice/autism-exclusion (accessed 15 Sept. 2021).

Davis, Alexandra. 'Making Church More Accessible', *Evangelical Alliance* (1 Jul. 2018) https://www.eauk.org/news-and-views/making-church-more-accessible (accessed 23 Jul. 2021).

Devlin, Hannah. 'Thousands of Autistic Girls and Women "Going Undiagnosed" due to Gender Bias', *The Guardian* (14 Sept. 2018) https://www.theguardian.com/society/2018/sep/14/thousands-of-autistic-girls-and-women-going-undiagnosed-due-to-gender-bias (accessed 31 Aug. 2021).

Dimensions (UK) Ltd, 'How often are disability hate crimes committed?' (2021) https://dimensions-uk.org/get-involved/campaigns/say-no-autism-learning-disability-hate-crime-imwithsam/know-more/often-disability-hate-crimes-committed/ (accessed 27 Jul. 2021).

Disability@Work, 'A tale of two commitments' (2017) https://www.disabilityatwork.co.uk/research-areas/disability-measurement-and-target/a-tale-of-two-commitments/ (accessed 16 Sept. 2021).

Durkin, Maureen S. et al. 'Autism Spectrum Disorder among US Children (2002–2010): Socioeconomic, Racial, and Ethnic Disparities', *American Journal of Public Health* (Nov. 2017), published online Oct. 2017.

Eiesland, Nancy L. *The Disabled God: Toward a Liberatory Theology of Disability* (Nashville: Abingdon Press, 1995).

Goldman, Ronald. *Readiness for Religion* (London: Routledge, 1969).

Kanner, Leo. 'Autistic Disturbances of Affective Contact', *Nervous Child* 2 (1943): pp. 217–50.

Kübler-Ross, Elisabeth. *On Death and Dying: What the Dying Have to Teach Doctors, Nurses, Clergy and Their Own Families* (London: Routledge, 2008).

Leniston, Tara and Rhian Grounds. *Coming Home to Autism: A Room-by-Room Approach to Supporting Your Child at Home after ASD Diagnosis* (London: Jessica Kingsley, 2018).

National Autistic Society, 'New shocking data highlights the autism employment gap' (19 Feb. 2021) https://www.autism.org.uk/what-we-do/news/new-data-on-the-autism-employment-gap (accessed 16 Sept. 2021).

Polanyi, Michael. *Personal Knowledge: Towards a Post-Critical Philosophy* (Abingdon: Routledge, 1998).

Pollack, Richard. *The Creation of Dr B: A Biography of Bruno Bettelheim* (New York: Simon & Schuster, 1996).

Rhodes, Giulia. 'Autism: A mother's labour of love', *The Guardian* (24 May 2011) https://www.theguardian.com/lifeandstyle/2011/may/24/autistic-spectrum-disorder-lorna-wing (accessed 29 July 2021).

Sellgren, Katherine. 'School Exclusion of Autistic Boy Unlawful, Judge Rules', *BBC News education report* (14 Aug. 2018) https://www.bbc.co.uk/news/education-45182213 (accessed 23 Jul. 2021).

Smith, Adam. 'Emotional Empathy in Autism Spectrum Conditions: Weak, Intact, or Heightened?' *Journal of Autism and Developmental Disorders* 39 (2009): pp. 1747–8.

Welby, Justin. *Dethroning Mammon: Making Money Serve Grace* (London: Bloomsbury, 2016).

Wing, Lorna and Judith Gould. 'Severe Impediments of Social Interaction and Associated Abnormalities in Children: Epidemiology and Classification', *Journal of Autism and Developmental Disorders* 9 (1979): pp. 11–29.

Reading, Viewing and Address List

There are a large number of books and articles on autism but you cannot read them all! Here is a personal selection of items that I have found helpful, apart from those I have already cited.

Baron-Cohen, Simon. *Autism and Asperger Syndrome* (Oxford: Oxford University Press: 2008).

Drew, Gillian. *An Adult with an Autism Diagnosis: A Guide for the Newly Diagnosed* (London: Jessica Kingsley, 2017).

Haddon, Mark. *The Curious Incident of the Dog in the Night-time* (London: Bloomsbury, 2004).

Hawkes, Hillary. *The Essential Guide to Asperger's Syndrome* (London: Essential Guide, 2017).

Higashida, Naoki. *Fall down Seven Times, Get up Eight* (trans. David Mitchell and K.A. Yoshida (London: Sceptre, 2017).

Higashida, Naoki. *The Reason I Jump* (trans. David Mitchell and K.A. Yoshida (London: Sceptre, 2014).

Hull, John et al. *Disability: The Inclusive Church Resource* (London: Dalton, Longman & Todd, 2014).

Normal, Henry and Angela Pell. *A Normal Family* (London: Two Roads, 2018).

Siclie-Kira, Chantal. *Autism Spectrum Disorders: The Complete Guide* (London: Verso, 2013).

Silverman, Steve. *Neurotribes* (London: Allen & Unwin, 2015).

Stuart, Keith. *A Boy Made of Blocks* (London: Sphere, 2016).

Terrell, Colin and Terri Passenger. *Understanding ADHD, Autism, Dyslexia and Dyspraxia* (London: Family Doctor, 2012).

Television programmes and films include:
  The A Word, BBC TV series
  Atypical, Netflix series
  Love on the Spectrum, Netflix series
  Marvellous, BBC film
  Forrest Gump, 1994 film
  Rain Man, 1988 film
  The Reason I Jump, 2021 film

This is an important address:
  The National Autistic Society
  393 City Road
  London EC1V 1NG
  Tel.: 08088 001 050

They publish *Your Autism Magazine*, which is an invaluable source of information about campaigns, equipment, research and how to support autistic people.

Authentic

We trust you enjoyed reading this book from Authentic. If you want to be informed of any new titles from this author and other releases you can sign up to the Authentic newsletter by scanning below:

Online:
authenticmedia.co.uk

Follow us:

Lightning Source UK Ltd.
Milton Keynes UK
UKHW051234030322
399453UK00008B/194